30-SECOND
MYTHOLOGY

30-SECOND
MYTHOLOGY

The 50 most important Greek and
Roman myths, monsters, heroes and gods,
each explained in half a minute

Editor
Robert A. Segal

Contributors
Viv Croot
Susan Deacy
Emma Griffiths
William Hansen
Geoffrey Miles
Barry B. Powell
Robert A. Segal

Ivy Press

First published in Great Britain in 2014 by

Ivy Press
210 High Street, Lewes,
East Sussex BN7 2NS, U.K.
www.ivypress.co.uk

British Library Cataloguing-in-
Publication Data
A CIP catalogue record for this
book is available from the
British Library.

ISBN 978-1-78240-096-7

Ivy Press
This book was conceived,
designed and produced by Ivy Press
Creative Director Peter Bridgewater
Publisher Jason Hook
Editorial Director Caroline Earle
Art Director Michael Whitehead
Designer Ginny Zeal
Illustrator Ivan Hissey
Profiles Text Viv Croot
Glossaries Text Steve Luck
Senior Editor Stephanie Evans
Project Editor Jamie Pumfrey

Typeset in Section

Printed in China

10 9 8 7 6 5 4 3 2 1

Distributed worldwide (except North America) by
Thames & Hudson Ltd., 181A High Holborn,
London WC1V 7QX, United Kingdom

CONTENTS

INTRODUCTION
Robert A. Segal

There is no uniform definition of 'myth'.

Instead, the numerous definitions reflect the various disciplines that study myths. As surprising as it sounds, a myth need not even be a story. For political scientists, a myth can instead be a belief or credo – an ideology. Even when myth is assumed to be a story, disciplines differ over the content. For folklorists, myths are exclusively about the creation of the world. All other stories constitute either legends or folktales. For other disciplines, myths can also be about the creation of a nation or a movement, or not be about the creation of anything. For the field of religious studies, the main characters in myths must be gods. Other disciplines, however, allow not only for heroes, who are human, but even for animals, who can sometimes be the outright creators of the world.

Three key questions

Many disciplines study myth – the chief ones being anthropology, sociology, psychology, political science, literature, philosophy and religious studies – and each discipline harbours multiple theories. To theorize about myth is to seek to answer three key questions, and to answer them for all myths, not just for a single myth or the myths of a single culture.

The key questions are those of origin, function and subject matter. 'Origin' addresses why and how myths arise whenever and wherever they do, not when and where they first arose. Function addresses why and how myths persist. The answer to the 'why' of both origin and function is usually a need, which the myth arises to fulfil and endures by continuing to fulfil. The need varies from theory to theory.

'Subject matter' addresses what the myth refers to – the 'referent'. Myths, it is popularly assumed, are to be read literally. Whether or not Zeus was real, myths about Zeus are supposed to be stories of a real god who was the chief god of mainstream, Homeric religion and who

Perseus slays the Gorgon
In one of the best-known heroic quests, Perseus travels to the home of the Gorgon sisters to behead Medusa. These epic tales have endured for centuries and still resonate with a modern audience.

used his power to do as he wished. However, myths can also be read symbolically, and the referent can be anything. Zeus, for example, can symbolize thunder and lightning, a king, a human father or even the fatherlike side of anyone's personality. Zeus need not be taken as a god, let alone the god of a long dead religion.

Theoretical shifts

Theories not only present myths but also make sense of them. Theories claim to know why myths ever arose, why they lasted for as long as they did, why they may still last and what they are really 'about'. One convenient distinction, which cuts across disciplines, is that between theories from the nineteenth century and theories from the twentieth.

Nineteenth-century theories – epitomized by those of E. B. Tylor and J. G. Frazer – usually saw the subject matter of myths as the physical world and the function of myths as either a literal explanation or a symbolic description of that world. Myths were taken to be the 'primitive' counterpart to natural science, which was assumed to be wholly or largely modern. Science rendered myths not merely redundant but outright incompatible, and modern audiences, which by definition were scientific, therefore had to reject myths.

By contrast, twentieth-century theories – typified by those of Bronislaw Malinowski, Mircea Eliade, Rudolf Bultmann, Albert Camus, Sigmund Freud and C. G. Jung – saw myths as anything but an outdated counterpart to science, either in subject matter or in function. (Nineteenth-century theorists like Friedrich Nietzsche foreshadowed this approach.) The subject matter was no longer the physical world but now was society, the human mind or the place of humans in the physical world. The function of myths was no longer explanation but now ranged from unifying the community, to encountering god, to encountering the unconscious, to expressing the human condition. In short, even in the wake of science, myths still had a place.

Enduring appeal

Did ancient Greeks and Romans believe literally in their mythology? Surprisingly, most did. Modern audiences may not share that literal belief, but the myths have endured and remain celebrated. Even if no one today considers Zeus or Achilles to be real, gods and heroes have flourished as symbols, of whom the grandest example is Dionysus.

Moreover, they have penetrated mainstream thought. Freud used the figure Oedipus to name the most fundamental human male drive, and Jung used the figure Electra to name its female counterpart.

Myths are to be found not only in Christianity and in ancient Greek and Roman religions but in most and maybe all other religions. Furthermore, myths need not be tied to any religion. Twentieth-century theories, in contrast to nineteenth-century ones, often severed myth from religion and studied secular myths, such as myths of nationalism or of outer space. Theories of myth are theories of all myths, not merely of any one culture or of any one kind.

Because classical myths are the best known, they are the focus of *30-Second Mythology*. The Greek, not Latin, names of the gods are used, but familiar Latin, or Roman, names are also given. Each mythological figure or event is first presented in a 30-second mythology, summarizing the key details for the reader, alongside a 3-second muse, which offers a more concise account. The 3-minute odyssey then goes into greater depth, outlining, for example, the symbolism contained within the myth, or further explaining its origin. Finally, related myths reveal the counterparts to mythical figures or events contained within other cultures and civilizations.

The seven chapters are divided into the categories of **Creation**, **Olympians**, **Monsters**, **Geography**, **Heroes**, **Tragic Figures** and **Legacy**, reflecting the way in which mythology pervades the whole classical world. Not only are there hundreds of gods, about many of whom there are multiple myths, but there also are mythic monsters, locations and events. The history of the cosmos begins with the creation of gods, who operate continually, often tragically, in the lives of humans. The hundreds of heroes themselves garner myths upon myths. These myths have persisted to this day, one of their legacies being the well-known psychological conditions that take their names from mythic figures.

Classical myths are to be found today in an array of places – not only in literature but also in the arts, the movies and not least popular culture. Modern versions of ancient myths invariably take liberties with the original stories, but what counts is that the myths, however updated, continue to be told.

CREATION

CREATION
GLOSSARY

adamantine sickle From 'adamant', which means extremely durable or hard. The most commonly referred to adamantine sickle in classical mythology is that made by Gaia and given to Cronus (Saturn), who used it to castrate his father, Uranus. There are, however, other references to adamantine sickles, such as the one Perseus used to kill Medusa and the sickle with which Zeus defeated Typhon.

cosmogony Derived from the Greek word *kosmos* (literally, 'order'), the term refers to the description, often to be found in myth, of the creation of the world.

Giants (Gigantes) The Giants were the huge, often monstrous, mortal male offspring of Gaia. She gave birth to the Giants, having been fertilized by Uranus' blood following his castration by Cronus. When the Olympians imprisoned the Titans, Gaia encouraged the Giants to wage war on Zeus and the other gods, hoping to overthrow them and to restore Titan supremacy. In the ensuing war (the Gigantomachy), Heracles, following a prophecy, was called upon by the gods to fight against the Giants. He personally killed a number of Giants and was responsible for the gods' ultimate victory.

Meliae A sisterhood of ash-tree nymphs (*melia* is Greek for ash), the Meliae, like the Giants and the Erinyes ('Furies'), were Gaia's offspring, fertilized by Uranus' blood. According to Hesiod in his *Works and Days*, the Meliae produced the third race of men, known as the Bronze Race, whom Hesiod described as being 'terrible and strong'.

Oceanids The collective name given to the many thousand sea nymph offspring of the Titans Oceanus and Tethys. Numbering between 3000 and 4000, they were closely associated with the seas and oceans, and many had individual names. Although not immortal, Oceanids lived for a very long time, and generally looked favourably on humans. They were often depicted playing around the keels and prows of boats.

Olympians The term generally refers to the 'Twelve Olympians' who gained control of the world after overthrowing the Titans in the war that has become known as the Titanomachy. The main gods of the Greek pantheon, the Twelve Olympians inhabited Mount Olympus, ruled by Zeus, god of the sky. The list of individual gods varies with the source, but the most widely accepted membership is Zeus, Hera, Poseidon, Demeter, Apollo, Artemis, Dionysus, Athena, Ares, Hephaestus, Hermes and Aphrodite.

Primordial Four In Greek cosmogony, the Primordial Four refers to the first four known entities. According to Hesiod in his *Theogony*, the first being to come into existence was Chaos, a 'vast and dark' chasm or abyss. After, but not out of, Chaos came Gaia ('earth mother'), followed by Tartarus (literally 'deep place'), a cosmic prison, and finally Eros (erotic love). As well as being physical things, the Primordial Four were also considered the earliest manifestations of gods.

Titanomachy The name given to the epic, ten-year war between the Titans and the Olympian gods. After overthrowing his tyrannical father, Uranus, Cronus became fearful that he too would be overthrown by his children. He swallowed them but was tricked into letting out Zeus, who was hidden and raised on Crete. Cronus was later forced to regurgitate his other children and, together with Zeus, the Giants and the Cyclopes (from whom Zeus received his trademark lightning bolt) battled the Titans, who were eventually defeated and cast into Tartarus.

underworld A general term used to describe the places that exist beneath the earth. The descriptions vary from one source to another, but the underworld in total included Tartarus, the cosmic prison of the Titans and the worst offending humans (particularly those, such as Tantalus and Sisyphus, who had offended the gods); Hades (or Erebus), where mortals went after death; and according to Virgil but not the Greek poets, Elysium (the Elysian Fields), the resting place of heroes. The most significant underworld river separating the living from the dead was the Styx, although it was across another river, Acheron, that Charon the ferryman carried the souls of the newly deceased.

CHAOS

the 30-second mythology

According to the early Greek

poet Hesiod, the first event to occur in the cosmos was the birth, or 'coming-into-being', of Chaos. After Chaos followed Gaia (earth), Tartarus (cosmic prison) and Eros (erotic love). These beings were the Primordial Four – the first four entities identified. Everything that came into the world thereafter derived ultimately from one or more of the Primordial Four. Chaos did not signify a state of utter disorder, as the word now implies; rather it was 'bounded space', as in a chasm. Indeed, the words 'chaos' and 'chasm' are etymologically related. In the logic of the myth Chaos offered room in which the world could develop. Chaos had a dual nature: it was not only a physical thing but also a personality, a living being out of which two other cosmic entities, Darkness and Night, emerged, which in turn produced other elements of the cosmos. Like Darkness and Night, the descendants of Chaos were mostly intangible elements such as Death, Sleep and Discord.

3-SECOND MUSE
Hesiod's cosmogony starts midway with Chaos but does not explain what preceded Chaos or what created Chaos.

3-MINUTE ODYSSEY
In the first century AD the Roman poet Ovid presented a different mythic cosmogony, in which the world initially consisted of shapeless matter, Chaos, within which reigned confusion and discord. Opposites warred with each other: heat with cold, wet with dry, hard with soft, heavy with light. Nature or some god liberated these elements, bringing order to the universe. In Ovid's version, Chaos was truly characterized by a state of 'utter disorder'.

RELATED MYTH
Many cosmogonic myths tell of an initial being or substance that contains within itself many of the eventual constituents of the cosmos. Examples are Tiamat (Mesopotamia) and Ginnungagap (Scandinavia).

3-SECOND BIOGRAPHIES
GAIA
Mother earth
See page 18

URANUS
Father sky
See page 22

HADES
Realm of the dead
See page 82

TARTARUS
Cosmic prison for defeated gods and monsters
See page 86

30-SECOND TEXT
William Hansen

The first being to come into existence, Chaos is a vast and dark chasm or abyss.

EROS/CUPID

the 30-second mythology

Eros was the Greek god of sexual attraction. His Roman counterpart was Cupid. In one account Eros was one of the Primordial Four entities. He embodied the creative urge of nature. In another version he was the child of the illicit liaison between Aphrodite and Ares. In an allegorical folktale Aphrodite, jealous of the sensationally beautiful Sicilian princess Psychê, told her son Eros to prick Psychê with his arrows and cause her to love a monster. In a mix-up Eros scratched himself, causing in him a hopeless passion for the girl. Eros spirited Psychê away to his home but remained invisible. They made love. Tricked by her envious sisters, Psychê lit a lamp and saw Eros; but burned by oil in the lamp, he flew away. Attempting to imitate Psychê's success, the sisters leapt from a mountain, expecting the West Wind (Zephyr) to carry them to Eros' abode. Instead, they were dashed on the rocks. Psychê searched everywhere for Eros and was tested by impossible tasks imposed on her by Aphrodite. However, Psychê was finally reunited with her beloved Eros, who married her and made her a goddess. Together, they had a daughter, Hedonê ('pleasure'). Apuleius' *Golden Ass* contains the classic Roman version of the story.

3-SECOND MUSE
Eros is the incarnation of sexual attraction, firing arrows that strike men and women alike, causing them to desire each other.

3-MINUTE ODYSSEY
In painting and sculpture Eros is portrayed as a nude winged boy or baby armed with a bow and a quiver of arrows. In ancient painting he is present with adults when there is sexual attraction among the humans. Psychê was the deification of the human soul, portrayed in ancient mosaics as a goddess with butterfly wings (*psychê* is also Greek for 'butterfly').

RELATED MYTH
Fertility gods can be either male or female, and are often paired together as in the case of Eros and Aphrodite.

3-SECOND BIOGRAPHIES
ARES/MARS
God of war, father of Eros
See page 40

APHRODITE/VENUS
Goddess of love and beauty
See page 50

30-SECOND TEXT
Barry B. Powell

Sometimes taken to be the product of an illicit affair between Aphrodite and Ares, Eros is the god of sexual desire.

GAIA

the 30-second mythology

'Broad-bosomed earth, sure standing-place' (in the early Greek poet Hesiod's words), Gaia emerged at the very beginning of creation, after Chaos. Developing from a living entity into an outright personality, Gaia gave virgin birth to Uranus, the 'sky father', then produced with him a mighty brood of children, headed by the Titans. In the strikingly Oedipal generational struggles of early Greek myth, Gaia's role is equivocal. When Uranus, fearful of his children, buried them back in her womb, Gaia gave her youngest son Cronus the adamantine sickle to castrate him; when Cronus in turn started swallowing his children, Gaia freed the youngest, Zeus, to use as a weapon against him. But when Zeus imprisoned his father, Gaia gave birth to the fearsome snaky monster Typhon to attack Zeus, only to make peace with Zeus and advise him how to counter the threat of his child Athena. Gaia's combination of the nurturing and the destructive reflected Greek male anxieties about female and maternal power. More fundamentally, Gaia was the earth itself, at once a beneficent and a ruthless mother, both womb and tomb for all the generations of earthly life.

3-SECOND MUSE
Gaia was the primordial 'earth mother', the oldest of goddesses – and for many the one most powerfully still with us today.

3-MINUTE ODYSSEY
Beginning in the 1970s, the scientist James Lovelock propounded what he called (at novelist William Golding's suggestion) the 'Gaia hypothesis' – the name reinforcing the concept of the earth as a single, complex, self-regulating, living organism, of which human beings are a part. While scientists continue to debate Lovelock's theory, Gaia remains a powerful figure for environmental and pagan movements.

RELATED MYTH
Almost all mythologies personify the earth as a mother goddess. The Egyptians are an exception, with a male earth (Geb) and female sky (Nut).

3-SECOND BIOGRAPHIES
CHAOS
The primordial cosmic entity with which creation began
See page 14

URANUS
The 'sky father', son and husband to Gaia
See page 22

THE TITANS
Children of Gaia and Uranus, the first generation of gods
See page 24

ZEUS/JUPITER
King of Olympus, god of the sky
See page 32

30-SECOND TEXT
Geoffrey Miles

Gaia is the primordial earth goddess and Zeus' grandmother.

c. 750/700 BC
Born

c. 700/650 BC
Composed *Theogony*

c. 700/650 BC
Composed *Works and Days*

c. 700/650 BC
Composed *Catalogue of Women*

1493
First printed edition of *Works and Days*

1495
Complete works published in Venice

1914
Works and Days and *Theogony* translated by Hugh G. Evelyn-White

1959
Hesiod: Works and Days, Theogony and *The Shield of Achilles* translated by Richmond Lattimore

HESIOD

Together with Homer, Hesiod

is one of the two fathers of Greek poetry.
Although he is the putative author of
numerous works, there are two that are
considered to be authentically his: *Works and
Days* and the *Theogony*. Whether a single
person composed these two works remains a
debated issue, just as the single authorship of
the *Iliad* and the *Odyssey* is still an unsettled
issue. Only a little is known about Hesiod
beyond what can be gleaned from internal
evidence. We do know that he bemoaned the
hardness and unfairness of life. Humans were
at the mercy of the gods, of the physical world
and of one another.

Hesiod had inherited from his father a small
patch of land at the foot of Mount Helicon,
the home of the Muses. His sheep pastured
on the lower slopes, and drank from one of
the sacred springs – the Hippocrene.

The *Theogony* is the main source of Greek
cosmogony, covering the creation, evolution
and descent of the gods and the eventual
hegemony of Zeus. *Works and Days* is

addressed to Hesiod's brother, Perses, with
whom he had a falling out over the division
of their father's estate. Where Hesiod was
prudent, Perses was profligate, and asked his
brother for a loan. In reply, Hesiod composed
Works and Days, which laments the injustice
of society and the hardness of life – too many
mouths to feed – but which also defends
the dignity of labour. *Works and Days* also
describes farming techniques as well as the
key myths of Prometheus and of Pandora and
the Ages – the alternative myths of the loss
of the equivalent of Paradise.

In contrast to Homer, who addresses kings
rather than ordinary persons, Hesiod addresses
fellow farmers and other commoners. Homer
and Hesiod, writing independently of each
other, nevertheless agree largely on the
constituents of the Pantheon, though they
differ on emphases and details. Together,
Homer and Hesiod constitute the equivalent
of the Greek Bible. Hesiod provides the myths
of creation and of the fall; Homer provides
subsequent human history.

URANUS

the 30-second mythology

According to Hesiod, Uranus was the son and then the husband of Gaia. He hated his offspring, pushing them down into a cranny of Gaia and thereby not allowing them to come forth. Gaia conspired with her son Cronus, a Titan, to overcome Uranus, giving Cronus an adamantine sickle (probably iron). Cronus waited in ambush from within Gaia. When Uranus came lusting for Gaia, Cronus cut off his father's genitals, which fell into the sea. The blood from the wound fell to the earth, whence sprang up the Giants ('earth-born ones'), the Erinyes (the 'Furies') and the Meliae (the ash-tree nymphs). From the foam gathered around the genitals that landed in the sea came forth Aphrodite (by false etymology, the 'foam-born one'). The story attributes creation to the separation or differentiation of either gods or elements – a common mythological process. Uranus and Gaia were, in effect, locked in a perpetual embrace, allowing no place for the world to appear. Once Uranus was castrated, the Titans and the other children of Uranus and Gaia could emerge, and the creation of the world could proceed.

3-SECOND MUSE
Uranus ('sky') was a primordial Greek god who arrested the progress of the world through his tyrannous sexual demands on Gaia ('earth').

3-MINUTE ODYSSEY
Hesiod's version beckons a psychoanalytic approach. There is the incestuous relationship between Uranus and Gaia – the son who becomes husband of his own mother, and in turn the father of their children. Then there is the Oedipal-like succession of Uranus by his son Cronus, and in turn of Cronus by his son Zeus.

RELATED MYTH
In Hittite myth Kumarbi bit off the genitals of his father, Anu, the sky god, became pregnant and (somehow) gave birth to the storm god Teshub, who deposed Kumarbi.

3-SECOND BIOGRAPHIES
CHAOS
The first primordial entity
See page 14

GAIA
Mother earth
See page 18

THE TITANS
Children of Gaia and Uranus
See page 24

30-SECOND TEXT
Barry B. Powell

Uranus, the primordial Greek sky god, is a sexual tyrant.

THE TITANS

the 30-second mythology

Gaia and Uranus gave birth to
the race of Titans, who warred unsuccessfully
against the Olympians in the great Titanomachy,
which lasted ten years. The meaning of 'Titan',
in spite of many suggestions, remains unclear.
In general, the Titans symbolized the powerful
forces of nature, untamed by the rational and
patriarchal rule of the Olympians. They were
seldom represented in art and garnered little
worship. Two notable Titans were the watery
male Oceanus and the female Tethys, probably
derived from the Babylonian watery Tiamat.
Oceanus was a river that surrounded the world.
According to Homer, Oceanus and Tethys gave
birth to all the other gods. Oceanus also fed all
the waters in wells, fountains and rivers. From
Oceanus and Tethys came the three thousand
Oceanids, spirits of the sea, rivers and springs.
Other Titans included Phoebe, who may be
connected with the sky, and Themis, who
represented that which is fixed and settled.
She controlled the Delphic Oracle before it
passed to Apollo and bore children to Zeus,
as did the Titan Mnemosyne, 'memory'.
Cronus and Rhea were parents or grandparents
of the Twelve Olympians, including Zeus.

3-SECOND MUSE
The Titans, whose power
was awesome, were the
children of Gaia and
Uranus, whom the
Olympians, under Zeus'
leadership, defeated in
a great battle.

3-MINUTE ODYSSEY
Iapetus and Themis
were the parents of
Prometheus, who, as
the son of a Titan himself,
had a long-running feud
with Zeus, who had
defeated and imprisoned
the other Titans. In
Hesiod's *Theogony*
and *Works and Days*
Prometheus is portrayed
as a trickster, whose
attempt to fool Zeus and
steal fire for mankind is
punished by an eagle
devouring his liver.

RELATED MYTH
Similar myths about a war
in heaven appear around the
world – for example, the Norse
wars between the Aesir and
Vanir, the Babylonian war
between Tiamat and Marduk
and the war between God and
Satan in Christian lore.

3-SECOND BIOGRAPHIES
PROMETHEUS
Rebel god, who stole fire
for mankind
See page 26

ZEUS/JUPITER
King of Olympus, god
of the sky
See page 32

TARTARUS
Prison of the Titans and also
the god of that prison
See page 86

30-SECOND TEXT
Barry B. Powell

*The Titans, the children
of Gaia and Uranus,
battled the Olympians
for control of the
world, but lost.*

PROMETHEUS

the 30-second mythology

3-SECOND MUSE
Prometheus was a rebel
god who championed the
interests of humankind
against those of the ruling
Olympian gods.

3-MINUTE ODYSSEY
Prometheus combines
two roles that are found
frequently in mythologies:
culture hero and trickster.
A culture hero facilitates
human civilization by
overcoming obstacles or
by giving humans basic
information or necessities,
as when Prometheus steals
fire from the gods for
humankind. A trickster
succeeds by cunning, as
when Prometheus deceives
Zeus into choosing the pile
of bones, as a result of
which humans get a better
portion of sacrificial
victims than gods do.

In the early days of the cosmos, the Olympian gods met with human males to decide how meat was to be apportioned between them. Prometheus, a son of the Titan god Iapetus, acted as facilitator. An ox was slaughtered, and Prometheus divided it into two piles. One consisted of meat covered with tripe, the other of bones covered with luscious fat. Prometheus invited the Olympian god Zeus to choose, and he selected the pile that looked good but that contained mostly bones. When Zeus perceived that he had been tricked, in his fury he withheld fire from mankind. So although men had meat, they could not cook it. (According to an alternative version, Zeus knew of the deceit but chose the inferior selection in order to punish humans later.) But Prometheus then stole fire from the gods and gave it to mankind. Zeus was now doubly angry, and so devised punishments for mankind as well as for mankind's divine champion. For mankind he invented womankind, ordering the craftsman god Hephaestus to fashion from clay the first woman, Pandora. She was foisted upon Prometheus' slow-witted brother, Epimetheus. As for Prometheus, Zeus had him bound to the side of a mountain, where an eagle daily tortured him by eating his liver.

RELATED MYTH
Culture heroes and tricksters in
myth are sometimes different
characters, sometimes a single
character. Coyote in Native
American cultures exemplifies
a character who combines
both roles.

3-SECOND BIOGRAPHIES
THE TITANS
Early family of gods
See page 24

ZEUS/JUPITER
King of the gods
See page 32

HEPHAESTUS/VULCAN
God of crafts
See page 38

HERMES/MERCURY
Messenger of the gods
See page 54

30-SECOND TEXT
William Hansen

*A wily rebel who
incurred Zeus' wrath
for stealing fire and
giving it to mankind,
Prometheus was
punished for his
impudence.*

OLYMPIANS

aegis A broad, ceremonial collar or garment (often supporting or carrying a shield) worn to demonstrate that protection was bestowed on the wearer by a divine power. The aegis dates back to Nubian and ancient Egyptian civilizations. In Greek mythology both Zeus and Athena are each described as wearing an aegis fashioned by Hephaestus, the divine craftsman. The word is now used to mean 'protection', as in, 'under the aegis of the United States'.

cult of Zeus The great oracle at Dodona in Epirus in northwest Greece was home to a cult of Zeus and is reputed to be the oldest oracle in Greece, dating back to the second millennium BC. Prophecies were given by bare-footed priests, known as the Helloi or Selloi, who divined the oracles by listening to the leaves of a sacred oak tree rustling in the breeze. Priestesses later replaced the priests. The shrine at Dodona is closely associated with Dione, who in some versions is a form of 'earth goddess'.

Curetes Cretan mountain spirits responsible for shepherding, hunting, beekeeping and metalwork. In Hesiod's *Theogony*, Gaia hid the child Zeus on Crete so that Cronus could not find him. She asked the Curetes to look after him – the sound of the child's cries were masked by their loud rituals. The Curetes, who worshipped Rhea, are often identified with the Phrygian Corybantes, who venerated the Phrygian counterpart Cybele.

Cyclopes The collective name for the group of one-eyed giants that appear at various times in Greek mythology. According to Hesiod's *Theogony*, the Cyclopes were one set of the children of Uranus and Gaia, who forged for Zeus the thunderbolt that was so effective in the Olympians' defeat of the Titans. The Cyclops Polyphemus, son of Poseidon, was famously tricked by Odysseus but was then avenged by his father.

Eleusinian Mysteries Sacred rituals held annually in the town of Eleusis, northwest of Athens, to honour the goddesses Persephone and Demeter. Believed to date back to the Mycenaean period, they were among the most significant ceremonies in the ancient Greek calendar and were a combination of secret initiation and celebration with, at their heart, the concept of death and rebirth. The festivities are believed to have lasted for around nine days during September, and were also closely associated with the sowing of crops – with Demeter as the goddess of grain and fertility.

mermen The male counterparts to mermaids. They were portrayed as bearded, with green hair and carrying a trident. They had a human head, arms and torso, but a fishlike tail instead of legs. The two most famous mermen in Greek mythology were Triton, the son of Poseidon, and Glaucus, a once mortal fisherman who was transformed into a merman after eating a magical plant.

omnipotent Although the gods in classical mythology were powerful, none of them was omnipotent, or all-powerful. Even Zeus was challenged by other gods, of whom he was often fearful, and unable to override Fate. The term is more accurately reserved for monotheistic religions. Yet even religions with a single god do not always deem that god to be omnipotent, which tends to be a philosophical, rather than popular, concept.

parthenogenesis (literally 'virgin birth') A form of asexual reproduction, and a common means of reproduction in the animal world, parthenogenesis was often found in classical mythology. Many of the key goddesses, from the primordial Gaia to Hera, wife and sister of Zeus, are capable of reproducing without sexual intercourse. The birth of Athena out of Zeus' head was not parthenogenetic since Athena had already been conceived with the goddess Metis. The term is also used to describe Jesus' birth.

psychopomp Name given to an entity that guides newly deceased souls to the next world or afterlife. There are numerous examples of psychopomps in classical mythology, notably Charon, Hermes, Hecate and Morpheus.

trident A large three-pronged spear associated with Poseidon (Neptune). Poseidon used his trident in a variety of ways, but primarily to create sources of water, to cause earthquakes and to conjure up storms. Mermen are also often depicted as carrying tridents.

ZEUS/JUPITER

the 30-second mythology

As well as the god of the sky,

Zeus was also the god of social customs – the protector of kings and of strangers. The Roman Jupiter was, even more, the embodiment of the state and its irresistible military power. Zeus was the youngest child of Cronus and Rhea. He was married to Hera, though he is famous for his amorous adventures that resulted in many offspring. Cronus sired children by his wife Rhea, but, like his father before him, he was a tyrant, swallowing the children as soon as they were born. When Zeus, Rhea's last child, was born, she instead gave Cronus a stone wrapped in swaddling clothes, which he unwittingly swallowed. Rhea secretly took the infant Zeus to Crete, where he was raised in a cave. Followers called Curetes beat their shields outside the cave to hide the infant's crying. When Zeus grew up, he overthrew Cronus and forced him to vomit up the children he had swallowed. There followed the Titanomachy, or battle against the Titans, in which, thanks to the thunderbolt manufactured by the Cyclopes, Zeus and the Olympians were victorious. Despite his supremacy Zeus was not omnipotent. He was challenged by other gods and was subject to Fate.

3-SECOND MUSE
Zeus (or Jupiter to the Romans) was the king of the gods, the head of the Olympian family – the 'father of gods and men', as Homer put it.

3-MINUTE ODYSSEY
At Dodona in Epirus, in remote northwest Greece, was a cult of Zeus centred on a sacred oak. There priestesses gave prophecies by listening to the rustling of the leaves of the oak tree. At Dodona Zeus' consort was Dione, a feminine form of Zeus, not Hera. Dione may have been Zeus' original consort before the Greeks arrived in the Balkan peninsula and took over a local cult of the mother goddess (that is, Hera).

RELATED MYTH
In Sanskrit there is a god Dyaus Pita, 'father Zeus', who is like the Greek/Roman god. In Norse myth the name of the god Tyr ('Tuesday') is based on the same Indo-European root.

3-SECOND BIOGRAPHIES
URANUS/SATURN
Father of the Olympians
See page 22

HERA/JUNO
Queen of the gods, wife of Zeus/Jupiter
See page 34

30-SECOND TEXT
Barry B. Powell

The youngest child of Cronus and Rhea, Zeus is the king of the gods and leads them to victory against the Titans. A prodigious lover, he fathers many gods and heroes.

HERA/JUNO
the 30-second mythology

3-SECOND MUSE
Hera, linked by the Romans with their marriage goddess Juno, was both Zeus' sister and queen.

3-MINUTE ODYSSEY
Zeus and Hera were hardly considered an old married couple, even though their marriage was made around the time of Zeus' rise to supremacy. This was because, after bathing annually at a sacred spring in Argos, Hera would renew her virginity and celebrate her marriage all over again. An ancient 'every woman', she was revered in Stymphalos as virgin, wife and – interestingly, in view of the immortal status of her husband – widow.

As one of the children of Cronus, the former ruler of the universe, Hera was never likely to be satisfied with second place, yet she played second-fiddle as the wife of her brother Zeus. She was, however, hardly a subservient wife, except on those occasions when Zeus was able to coerce her into submission with threats of domestic violence. And well she might have been frightened: her husband had once hung her from the summit of Olympus by her wrists with her feet weighted down by anvils. Most often, however, her anger was directed at the various lovers and illegitimate children of Zeus rather than at the god himself. Heracles, the greatest of Zeus' mortal offspring, was the most persistently persecuted until he died. After he was made immortal, Hera gave him her daughter Hebe as wife. Unlike her husband, she took no lovers. At the same time she was capable of having children without him. Her response to his production of Athena out of his own head, though only after intercourse with the goddess Metis, was to give birth to Hephaestus by parthenogenesis ('maiden-birth'), that is, entirely by herself. In a Roman take on this story, after Minerva appeared out of Jupiter's head, Flora gave Juno a magical herb to impregnate her with Mars.

RELATED MYTH
As the Queen of Olympus, Hera shared some traits of the Phoenician great goddess Astarte, and of the Mesopotamian Ishtar.

3-SECOND BIOGRAPHIES
ZEUS/JUPITER
King of Olympus, god of the sky
See page 32

HEPHAESTUS/VULCAN
God of crafts, blacksmith to the gods
See page 38

ARES/MARS
God of war, son of Zeus and Hera
See page 40

HERACLES/HERCULES
Greek hero of immense strength
See page 96

30-SECOND TEXT
Susan Deacy

Hera is locked in a conflict-ridden marriage with Zeus, whose infidelities fuel repeated acts of vindictive persecution.

POSEIDON/NEPTUNE

the 30-second mythology

3-SECOND MUSE
Son of the Titans Cronus and Rhea, Poseidon – identified with the Roman god Neptune – was the powerful god of the sea, earthquakes and horses.

3-MINUTE ODYSSEY
In punishment for a disagreement, Zeus forced Poseidon and Apollo to serve King Laomedon of Troy. Laomedon ordered them to build Troy's massive walls but then refused to pay them as he had promised. To punish the Trojans, Poseidon sent a great sea monster against the city. Heracles killed it in return for Laomedon's daughter. Poseidon was the divine enemy of Odysseus because he blinded his son, the Cyclops Polyphemus. Poseidon delayed Odysseus' return home to Ithaca for ten years.

Together with his brothers, Zeus and Hades, Poseidon cast lots for sovereignty over the world. Zeus took the sky, Hades the underworld and Poseidon the sea. Poseidon's emblem was the trident, a three-pronged spear with which he could strike the ground, causing springs to emerge. His most significant consort, of whom there were many, was the sea nymph Amphitrite, and together they had a merman son, Triton. When Poseidon and Athena competed for sponsorship of the city of Athens, Poseidon struck the Acropolis with his trident, and a salt spring burst forth. Athena, however, planted an olive tree and was chosen by the Athenians as their civic deity. In revenge, Poseidon flooded the plain of Attica, on which Athens stands. Poseidon was the father of Theseus and of many other heroes, but some of his children were more than human. In one myth Poseidon courted the goddess Demeter, but his love was not reciprocated. To avoid him she turned herself into a mare. Poseidon, however, became a stallion and covered her; their offspring was the magical horse Arion. Unlike other primordial water gods, Poseidon is a fully-fledged personality, and one separate from the natural phenomenon he controls.

RELATED MYTH
Other mythological water gods are the Egyptian Nun and the Babylonian Tiamat.

3-SECOND BIOGRAPHIES
POLYPHEMUS
The Cyclops son of Poseidon
See page 68

ODYSSEUS/ULYSSES
King of Ithaca whose Trojan Horse led to Troy's downfall
See page 102

THESEUS
Hero of Athens, son of Poseidon
See page 106

30-SECOND TEXT
Barry B. Powell

The god of the sea, like his brother Zeus, engages in numerous sexual conquests. Poseidon's emblem is the trident.

HEPHAESTUS/ VULCAN

the 30-second mythology

Hephaestus was depicted as

either the son of Zeus and Hera, or of Hera alone. In this version, his mother conceived him spontaneously to take revenge on her husband when he gave birth to Athena. That it is Hephaestus who in some versions facilitates the birth of Athena provides a further instance of mythological flexibility, as does the question of how Hephaestus became lame. Either Hera's horror at producing a disabled child led her to hurl him off Olympus, or it was the fall that caused the disability. Hephaestus' lameness marginalized him on Olympus, however much his fellow deities needed the gifts that he was uniquely qualified to provide. As well as equipping the gods with their various weapons and other attributes, he helped particular Olympians to get out of certain tricky situations. When, for example, Athena was stuck, fully developed, inside the head of Zeus, it was the axe blow of Hephaestus that released her. His skill at craft also enabled him to turn particular situations to his favour, as when his unfaithful wife, Aphrodite, found herself caught with her lover Ares in a net so fine that it looked invisible.

3-SECOND MUSE
Hephaestus – identified with the Roman god Vulcan – was the divine craftsman, whose talent at fashioning intricate objects was regarded as unrivalled.

3-MINUTE ODYSSEY
As well as creating such wondrous, not to mention indestructible, objects as Athena's aegis, Aphrodite's girdle and the armour of Achilles, Hephaestus was also responsible for creations that were so cleverly constructed that they appeared to be alive. He was also key to the creation of specific human beings, including Pandora – the first woman – and Erichthonius, through whom Athenians could claim the status of 'children of Hephaestus'.

RELATED MYTH
Hephaestus shares traits with several clever gods often known as 'tricksters', for example, Enki of the Sumerians and a range of Native American figures.

3-SECOND BIOGRAPHIES
ZEUS/JUPITER
King of Olympus, god of the sky
See page 32

HERA/JUNO
Queen of the gods, wife of Zeus/Jupiter
See page 34

APHRODITE/VENUS
Goddess of love and beauty
See page 50

ATHENA/MINERVA
Goddess of wisdom, warfare and justice
See page 52

30-SECOND TEXT
Susan Deacy

Known for his skill, craftsmanship and ingenuity, the lame Hephaestus is married to the goddess of love, Aphrodite.

ARES/MARS

The name for the Roman god

Mars may derive from the same root as Ares, the Greek god of war, but Mars represented heroic valour while Ares represented the violence and bloodlust of war. Ares was thus very different from Athena, who espoused military intelligence and strategic thinking. Outright opposite to Ares was Aphrodite, the goddess of love. Yet the two became lovers, even though she was married to the crippled god Hephaestus, whom she despised. The sun god Helios, who sees all, informed Hephaestus of the affair, and so the craftsman god contrived a trap of a fine golden mesh suspended over the wedding bed. He told his wife that he was going to Lemnos, but he soon returned to catch Ares in bed with Aphrodite. He sprang the trap, and the net imprisoned the naked gods. All the other Olympians came to look and sneer, but the goddesses held back for modesty. At last the lovers were freed. Ares went to Thrace, his homeland, and Aphrodite went to Paphos in Cyprus, the site of her birth. Deimos ('terror') and Phobos ('fear') were the offspring of Ares and Aphrodite, and today give their names to two moons of the planet Mars.

3-SECOND MUSE
One of the Olympians, Ares ('battle' or 'curse') was the god not merely of war, but of slaughter and bloodlust, in which he delighted.

3-MINUTE ODYSSEY
Ares took the side of Troy in the epic Trojan War. Yet despite all his power, such as when entering the body of Hector and forcing back the Greek lines almost single-handedly, he was not able to secure victory for the Trojans. In his book *Civilization and its Discontents*, Freud sees love and war (aggression) as the key drives in humans, and sees them as opposed, just as Aphrodite and Ares are.

RELATED MYTH
The Norse god Tyr, the god of war, was akin to Ares. From the name Tyr comes our 'Tuesday'. He was, however, surpassed in fighting by Odin, or Wotan, the chief of the Norse gods and one compared with Zeus. From the name Wotan comes our 'Wednesday'.

3-SECOND BIOGRAPHIES
HEPHAESTUS/VULCAN
God of craftsmen
See page 38

APHRODITE/VENUS
Goddess of love and beauty
See page 50

30-SECOND TEXT
Barry B. Powell

Ares' lust for battle stands opposite to Aphrodite's devotion to love and beauty, yet the two were lovers.

APOLLO

the 30-second mythology

The ever youthful Apollo was

the son of Zeus and Leto, and was the twin brother of Artemis. Before being integrated into the Olympian family, Apollo was feared by the regions of the earth and by the gods. Only Delos – a floating island that could claim not to be, strictly, a 'land' – was willing to host his birth. Seeming to bear out a prophecy that he would 'greatly lord it among gods and mortal men' (*Homeric Hymn to Apollo* 68–9), Apollo, upon arriving at the house of Zeus, stretched his bow. In fear, the other gods left their thrones till Leto disarmed him. Apollo's achievements included his victory over the serpent Python, the previous ruler of Delphi. The site thereafter became his foremost place of worship. In response to slights upon his mother's honour, Apollo took joint vengeance with his twin sister and fellow archer, Artemis. When Niobe boasted that she was more fertile than Leto, the pair shot and killed her children. Among his other deeds were ones for which he incurred punishment. For slaying the Cyclopes, for instance, Zeus made him spend a year tending the livestock of the mortal Admetus.

3-SECOND MUSE
Apollo, who came to be identified with the sun god Helios, was the patron of many things, including poetry, prophecy, music, medicine and plagues.

3-MINUTE ODYSSEY
Apollo preached, but did not always practise, moderation in life. On several occasions, his attempts to deflower females failed. For example, Cassandra retained her virginity as did her fellow prophetess, the Sibyl of Cumae; meanwhile, Daphne escaped rape through transformation into a laurel. These failures notwithstanding, Apollo was the father of several children, including the healing god Asclepius (by Coronis), the herdsman Aristaeus (by Cyrene) and Ion, the product of his rape of Creusa.

RELATED MYTH
The Near Eastern god who bears closest similarity to Apollo is the Hurrian plague deity, Aplu.

3-SECOND BIOGRAPHY
ZEUS/JUPITER
King of Olympus, god of the sky
See page 32

30-SECOND TEXT
Susan Deacy

This god of music, good health and the sun was at the same time a vengeance-seeking, plague-bringing god, some of whose beloveds, like his enemies, came to unfortunate ends.

Eighth century BC
Homer active?

750 BC
The *Iliad*, then *Odyssey* composed – both prior to Hesiod

Second century BC
'Stabilized' text of both poems composed in Alexandria

15th century
Homer rediscovered in Renaissance Italy

1488
The first printed edition of the *Iliad* and the *Odyssey*

1675–1676
Thomas Hobbes' translation of both works published

1700
John Dryden's version of the *Iliad* published

1898–1900
The *Iliad* and the *Odyssey* translated by Samuel Butler

1961
The *Iliad* translated by Richard Lattimore

1989
The *Iliad* translated by Robert Fitzgerald

1998
The *Odyssey* translated by Robert Fitzgerald

HOMER

Although he is among the best- known ancient Greek poets and the author of two of the most influential epic poems in Western literature – the *Iliad* and the *Odyssey* – little is known about Homer. He might have been born on the island of Chios, or at Smyrna on the coast of Turkey. There was an ancient tradition that he was blind (in some dialects the word *omeros* is associated with blindness). Herodotus was insistent that Homer predated him by some 400 years, which puts Homer at around 850 BC. Others maintain that Homer was an eyewitness (blind or sighted) to the Trojan War and therefore must have lived in the twelfth century BC. A third possibility is that there was more than one Homer, just as there might have been more than one Hesiod. The ancients almost uniformly assumed a single Homer, and the suggestion of multiple authors became popular only as part of the rise of modern critical approaches to ancient texts of all kinds. The problems of the authorship of more than one work are common, such as with the many letters attributed to St Paul. One of Homer's famous translators, Samuel Butler, argued that Homer might have been a woman.

While scholars in the twentieth century came mostly to return to the ancient view of a single Homer, everyone grants that the two works present differing views of the relations among the gods and of the relations between gods and humans. Still, both works assume a common view of the place of the gods and of Fate in human affairs. Both works emphasize the unhappy nature of life after death in Hades. At the same time, both works stress the need for the burial of the dead. Above all, both works, though especially the *Iliad*, are about aristocrats and not about ordinary Greeks or Trojans.

Both epics, like other ancient works, were originally oral and were written down only later. Some scholars maintain that the works were standardized in the eighth century BC, others that they became standardized in the seventh century BC and were written down in the sixth century. The Greek alphabet was established in the eighth century BC, so the poems could not have been written down any earlier. Doubtless the *Iliad*, which is about the origin and the last year of the Trojan War, was composed earlier than the *Odyssey*, which is about Odysseus' return home following the end of the war. But who Homer was and, even now, how many Homers there were are questions still debated by classicists.

ARTEMIS/DIANA

the 30-second mythology

3-SECOND MUSE
Artemis was the virgin goddess of the forest, known to Homer as *potnia Thêrôn*, 'mistress of the wild animals'. She presided over the hunt, childbirth and the sudden death of women.

3-MINUTE ODYSSEY
Artemis was an ally of the Trojans. When the Greek King Agamemnon killed a stag in her sacred grove and then boasted that he was a better hunter than Artemis, she required the sacrificial death of his daughter Iphigenia before she would allow the winds to bear the Greeks to Troy. According to one version, at the last minute she substituted a deer for the girl, whom she carried to the Crimea to serve as her priestess.

Artemis, identified by the

Romans with Diana, was the very dangerous goddess of the hunt, wild animals, wilderness and later the moon. She was responsible for the mysterious deaths of women. Her parents were Zeus and the nymph Leto, and she is often shown with her bow and arrows and her twin brother Apollo, who was her constant companion. Hera, furious at Zeus' infidelity with Leto, commanded that she could give birth on no place 'that saw the light of day'. Delos, at the centre of the Cyclades, was a floating island, bobbing beneath the surface. There the suffering Leto gave birth to Artemis, who then immediately helped to deliver her brother. She was thus recognized as protecting women in childbirth. When Artemis was bathing, the hunter Actaeon saw her naked. Offended and ashamed, she transformed him into a stag. Actaeon's own dogs, not recognizing their master, tore him to pieces. Niobe thought she was better than Leto because she had seven boys and seven girls, whereas Leto gave birth only to Artemis and Apollo. In response, Apollo killed her sons with his arrows, and Artemis shot her daughters. Devastated, Niobe turned into a stone that even now is said to weep in the mountains of western Turkey.

RELATED MYTH
The Thracian goddess Bendis, also a goddess of the moon and hunting, is closely associated with Artemis and Diana.

3-SECOND BIOGRAPHIES
APOLLO
God of prophecy and the sun
See page 42

ACTAEON
Hunter who saw Artemis naked
See page 134

30-SECOND TEXT
Barry B. Powell

Artemis is Apollo's sister and the goddess of hunting. Unlike most Olympians, she is strictly chaste.

DEMETER/CERES

the 30-second mythology

The daughter of Cronus and Rhea, Demeter (meaning 'earth mother') was one of the earliest Olympians. She oversaw the growth of crops and all aspects of fertility, including childbirth. Her daughter, Persephone (Roman Proserpina), was abducted by Hades and became queen of the underworld. Grief-stricken, Demeter stopped all growth across the earth. As she searched for her daughter, she disguised herself as an old woman. She spent some time in Eleusis, where, in gratitude, she tried to bestow immortality on the king's infant son, Demophon – an effort that backfired. She continued her search until she discovered Persephone's whereabouts and demanded her release. As a compromise, Zeus allowed Persephone to spend part of the year with Demeter and part with Hades, providing a mythological reason for the changing seasons. In a more sublime sense, Demeter and Persephone were worshipped in the Eleusinian Mysteries (secret initiation ceremonies) as goddesses who eased the transition between life and death. Although she was generally seen as a benevolent figure, she could be dangerous if insulted. When Erysichthon cut down trees in her sacred grove, Demeter punished him with an insatiable craving for food. He ate and ate but remained insatiable.

3-SECOND MUSE
Demeter, known to the Romans as 'Ceres', was goddess of the harvest and fertility, and was seen as a second goddess of the earth itself.

3-MINUTE ODYSSEY
Demeter was unlucky in love. She gave birth to Persephone after sleeping with Zeus, but when Demeter fell in love with Iasion and bore him a son, Ploutos, Zeus killed Iasion out of jealousy. Demeter's problems continued while searching for Persephone. She was pursued by her brother Poseidon, and when she was transformed into a horse to escape, Poseidon changed into a stallion. The ensuing liaison resulted in the birth of an immortal horse, Arion.

RELATED MYTH
Adonis was also fought over by gods – specifically goddesses – and joint custody had to be granted by Zeus. Primordial mother figures are found in many mythologies, from the Egyptian Isis to the Inuit Aakuluujjusi.

3-SECOND BIOGRAPHIES
ZEUS/JUPITER
King of Olympus, god of the sky
See page 32

POSEIDON/NEPTUNE
God of the sea and of horses
See page 36

DIONYSUS/BACCHUS
God of wine, son of Zeus
See page 56

HADES
The underworld, and the name given to its king
See page 82

30-SECOND TEXT
Emma Griffiths

Demeter is an earth mother, whose annual separation from her daughter is supposed to explain the changing seasons.

APHRODITE/VENUS

the 30-second mythology

3-SECOND MUSE
Aphrodite was the Greek goddess of love, beauty and harmony. She was known to the Romans as Venus.

3-MINUTE ODYSSEY
Aphrodite's best-known example of interfering with mortal destiny occurred during the Trojan War. Aphrodite, Athena and Hera held a contest to see who was the most beautiful. Zeus declined to decide and instead pressured the Trojan prince Paris into making the judgment. All three offered bribes for his vote, with Aphrodite winning him over by the promise of the most beautiful woman in the world. Following her victory, Aphrodite gave him Helen, who was already married to the Greek King Menelaus. War with Troy was inevitable.

Aphrodite means 'born of foam' (from the Greek *aphros*). She was created when the Titan Cronus threw the mutilated genitals of his father, Uranus, into the sea, where they foamed and boiled, and out of which, on the shores of Cyprus, appeared Aphrodite – a beautiful, young woman, carried on a scallop shell. An alternative version maintains that she was the daughter of Zeus and Dione, an avatar of the earth goddess. Aphrodite can be taken as either the source or the manifestation of the overwhelming and often destructive power of love. Realizing that her beauty would bring trouble, Zeus married her to the ugly and crippled Hephaestus, who, rather counterproductively, created for her a magical, jewelled girdle that made her even more irresistible. Aphrodite had affairs with gods and mortals indiscriminately. She enjoyed liaisons with the mortal Trojan prince Anchises, resulting in the birth of Aeneas, and with the god Hermes, resulting in the birth of Hermaphroditus. She also had a long dalliance with Adonis. Her longest affair was with Ares (Mars), out of which she gave birth to Eros, the armed god of sexual desire whose indiscriminate arrows explain or express the capriciousness and painfulness of love.

RELATED MYTH
Parallel to Aphrodite are the goddesses Astarte (Phoenician), Hathor (Egyptian), Inanna (Babylonian), Ishtar (Akkadian) and Freya (Norse).

3-SECOND BIOGRAPHIES
ZEUS/JUPITER
King of Olympus, god of the sky
See page 32

HERA/JUNO
Queen of Olympus, consort to Zeus
See page 34

HEPHAESTUS/VULCAN
God of crafts, blacksmith to the gods
See page 38

ARES/MARS
God of war, son of Zeus and Hera
See page 40

30-SECOND TEXT
Viv Croot

The goddess of beauty, pleasure, love and procreation beguiles gods and mortals alike.

ATHENA/MINERVA

the 30-second mythology

Athena was born as a by-product

of Zeus' attempt to retain his throne after hearing that the son born to his first wife, Metis, would unseat him. His response was to swallow Metis, who was pregnant with Athena at the time. The child remained stuck inside Zeus until an axe-wielding Hephaestus or, in some versions, Prometheus struck open his head and the fully-grown Athena leapt out, wearing flashing armour, to the astonishment of the assembled gods. Cosmic chaos ensued until, by removing her weapons, Athena restored normality. Athena took possession of her favourite city, Athens, when her gift of the first olive tree was preferred to the salt spring created by her rival, Poseidon. Her tie to Athens was strengthened through her involvement in the birth of Erichthonius, one of its ancestral heroes. When she went to Hephaestus to ask him to make weapons, he attempted to rape her. During their struggle Hephaestus' semen fell to the ground and a child, Erichthonius ('very-earthy'), emerged from the fertilized earth. Gaia, the earth goddess, handed the child to Athena, who then reared him. Athena was credited with numerous inventions, including the flute, the ship, the horse-bit, the plough and the chariot.

3-SECOND MUSE
Athena – identified with the Roman goddess Minerva – was at once a warrior-maiden, city-protectress, mother, craftsperson, helper of heroes and inventor.

3-MINUTE ODYSSEY
Athena was the patron of so many heroes that one might say that one of the qualifications for heroism was to have her on one's side. An array of males – including Heracles, Perseus, Odysseus and Jason – flourished under her protection. Her wrath was equally effective, as the Greeks discovered when, after the sack of Troy, they failed to punish the lesser Ajax for the rape of Cassandra at Athena's sacred image, the Palladium.

RELATED MYTH
Athena is akin to other warrior goddesses, including the Hittite sun goddess of Arinna and the Hindu deity Durga.

3-SECOND BIOGRAPHIES
ZEUS/JUPITER
King of Olympus, god of the sky
See page 32

HERACLES/HERCULES
Greek hero of immense strength
See page 96

ODYSSEUS/ULYSSES
Greek hero whose Trojan Horse defeated Troy
See page 102

PERSEUS
Greek hero who killed Medusa
See page 108

30-SECOND TEXT
Susan Deacy

The warrior-maiden Athena is the patron of numerous cities and many heroes.

HERMES/MERCURY
the 30-second mythology

As shining, slippery and mercurial as the liquid metal to which he gave his (Roman) name, Hermes was the messenger of the gods. Flying between Olympus and earth on the wings of his broad-brimmed hat and sandals, and carrying his snake-entwined herald's rod (the caduceus), he took messages to mortals from his father, Zeus. Sometimes he brought help, as when he showed Odysseus the magic herb that saved him from Circe's enchantment. Other times he brought stern divine commands, as when he told Aeneas to leave Dido and establish the future site of Rome. Talker, trader, traveller, trickster and thief, Hermes presided over all forms of exchange and communication. His skill with words made him the patron of writers and orators, of academics and diplomats. He saw to the circulation of goods by merchants and thieves (not that dissimilar, in the ancient Greeks' view), and watched over travellers and border crossers. As he himself crossed the boundary between heaven and earth, he also crossed the one between life and death. As psychopomp, or spirit guide, he conducted the souls of the dead to Hades – and, very occasionally, back again. In the Hellenistic period Hermes became associated with wisdom, hence the term 'hermeneutics': the study of the principles of interpretation.

3-SECOND MUSE
Hermes was the light-footed, light-fingered and smooth-tongued messenger of the gods, known to Romans as Mercury.

3-MINUTE ODYSSEY
The Homeric Hymn to Hermes celebrates the god as child prodigy. When he was only one day old, he leapt from his cradle and stole a herd of cattle from his half-brother Apollo, who remained unconvinced by Hermes' protestations that he was only an innocent baby. But Hermes pacified Apollo by the gift of a musical instrument that he had just invented out of a tortoise shell – the lyre.

RELATED MYTH
Hermes and the Egyptian god Thoth are combined in the figure of the wise Hermes Trismegistus. The Celtic Ogmios is a god of eloquence and is also a psychopomp.

3-SECOND BIOGRAPHIES
ZEUS/JUPITER
King of Olympus, god of the sky
See page 32

APOLLO
God of light, music and poetry
See page 42

HADES
The name of both the underworld and its king
See page 82

ODYSSEUS/ULYSSES
Greek warrior, traveller and trickster
See page 102

30-SECOND TEXT
Geoffrey Miles

More than simply a messenger, Zeus' fleet-footed son is the original 'mercurial' genius.

DIONYSUS/BACCHUS
the 30-second mythology

A figure connected with both physical and social phenomena, Dionysus was associated with wine, ecstasy, communality, mystery cult and death. Classical Dionysiac myths communicate the joys of a god who, according to one epithet, was the 'Liberator' (Eleutherios). Under his power, women rushed to the mountainside, and men practised hedonism. The various disastrous attempts to resist Dionysus are illustrated by the punishment meted out to Pentheus, Dionysus' cousin, who was torn apart by his mother and aunts. Meanwhile the daughters of Minyas, who remained at their looms after their fellow Boeotian women had dashed off to the mountainside in bacchic frenzy, came themselves to be so thoroughly inspired by Dionysian madness that, in some versions, they tore apart one of their own children. Distraught, they roamed the mountain until Hermes transformed them into bats. As the 'twice born' god, Dionysus was torn from the womb of Semele as she was being incinerated by Zeus' lightning. The foetus was sewn into the thigh of Zeus, out of which the god was eventually born. He was born yet again after the Titans dismembered him, Athena producing a reconstructed Dionysus from the still-beating heart.

3-SECOND MUSE
Dionysus, the 'most terrible, and most gentle, to humankind', has survived more fully as a symbol of one side of human nature than have most other ancient gods.

3-MINUTE ODYSSEY
In the nineteenth century stories of Dionysus' arrival from the East were thought to explain away why the Greeks worshipped a deity supposedly at odds with the rationality for which they were famed. Since the discovery of a being named DI-WO-NI-SO-JO on the Mycenaean Greek Linear B tablets, it has become clear his worship goes back at least to the Bronze Age.

RELATED MYTH
Dionysus' mixed parentage, his connections with wine and mystery, and his death and rebirth all led to the suggestion of parallels with the life of Jesus.

3-SECOND BIOGRAPHIES
THE TITANS
Children of Gaia and Uranus
See page 24

ZEUS/JUPITER
King of Olympus, god of the sky
See page 32

HEPHAESTUS/VULCAN
God of crafts, blacksmith to the gods
See page 38

ATHENA/MINERVA
Goddess of wisdom, warfare and justice
See page 52

30-SECOND TEXT
Susan Deacy

From wine to ecstasy to death, Dionysus' array of responsibilities may explain his enduring appeal.

MONSTERS

aegis A broad, ceremonial collar or garment (often supporting or carrying a shield) worn to demonstrate that protection was bestowed on the wearer by a divine power. The aegis dates back to Nubian and ancient Egyptian civilizations. In Greek mythology both Zeus and Athena are each described as wearing an aegis fashioned by Hephaestus, the divine craftsman. The word is now used to mean 'protection', as in, 'under the aegis of the United States'.

Argonauts Named after the ship in which they sailed, the *Argo*, the Argonauts were a group of heroic adventurers who joined Jason on his voyage to Colchis on the shores of the Black Sea in search of the Golden Fleece. The number of Argonauts varies from source to source, but around fifty is the most common figure, and among them were some of the most famous ancient heroes, notably Heracles, Orpheus and Theseus.

Chimaera Greek mythological monster that had the body of a lioness, a tail that ended with a snake's head, and a goat's neck and head emerging from its back. Capable of breathing fire, the monster was usually portrayed as female. According to Hesiod, she was the offspring of Echidna.

Cyclopes The collective name given to the group of one-eyed giants that appear at various times in Greek mythology. According to Hesiod in the *Theogony*, the Cyclopes were three primordial sons of Uranus and Gaia who forged for Zeus the thunderbolt that was so decisive in the Olympians' defeat of the Titans. The best-known Cyclops was Polyphemus, the son of Poseidon, who was famously tricked by Odysseus.

labyrinth In Greek mythology, an extraordinarily complex construction of corridors. It was designed by Daedalus on behalf of King Minos of Crete and was built to imprison the Minotaur, a man with a bull's head. The location of the labyrinth is not known, although there are some who believe that it may have been on the site of the Knossos palace complex, a theory that was inspired by travellers' reports describing the intricate layout of the palace.

metamorphosis The transformation of one object into another; in mythology usually a human into an animal or plant. Ancient Greek mythology is full of examples of metamorphoses, often either undertaken deliberately by a god or goddess in order to fulfil a personal quest or ambition, such as Zeus turning himself into a swan in order to seduce Leda, or enacted on a mortal by a god or goddess as a form of punishment, as when Artemis turned Actaeon into a stag. It has been suggested that the myths of metamorphoses in early religions served to explain the transformation from one species to another.

underworld A general term used to describe the place that exists beneath the earth. The descriptions and realms are fluid from one source to another, but the underworld often comprised Tartarus, the cosmic prison of the Titans and of the worst human offenders; Hades (or Erebus), where mortals went after death; and Elysium (the Elysian Fields), the resting place of heroes. The most significant underworld river separating the living from the dead was the Styx, although it was across another river, Acheron, that Charon the ferryman carried the souls of the newly deceased.

THE MINOTAUR

the 30-second mythology

The Minotaur, rarely remembered by his name Asterion (the 'starry one'), was the result of King Minos' hubris. In the grip of a fraternal power struggle for the throne of Crete, Minos appealed to Poseidon. The god sent him a white bull from the sea, which Minos was to sacrifice. It was such a splendid beast that the king kept it for himself and sacrificed a lesser animal instead. In revenge, Poseidon asked Aphrodite to make Minos' wife, Pasiphae, fall hopelessly in love with the bull, which she did. She then commanded Daedalus to build a wooden cow into which she could climb to consummate her passion. She suckled the resultant bull-headed child, the Minotaur, but when it became too wild and aggressive, Minos ordered Daedalus to build the labyrinth to imprison it. Through political machinations, Minos was able to demand tribute from Aegeus, King of Athens, in the form of a supply of maidens and youths to feed the Minotaur. After three years, the Athenian hero Theseus volunteered to be part of the tribute. With the help of Ariadne, Minos' daughter, and a ball of twine to mark the route, he fought and killed the Minotaur, cut off its head and escaped from the labyrinth.

3-SECOND MUSE
With the body of a man and the head of a bull, the Minotaur was the offspring of Pasiphae, wife of Minos of Crete, and a white bull.

3-MINUTE ODYSSEY
Minos/Minotaur is sometimes taken as the embodiment of the Cretan sun god, who is usually depicted as a bull. Crete has always been associated with bulls. When Zeus fell in love with the Phoenician princess Europa, he disguised himself as a white bull, lured her onto his back and then swam off with her to Crete.

RELATED MYTH
In Japanese classical literature the ushi-oni is a bull-headed demon. It takes various forms but is typically a horned and ferocious monster.

3-SECOND BIOGRAPHIES
POSEIDON/NEPTUNE
God of the sea and horses, brother to Zeus
See page 36

APHRODITE/VENUS
Goddess of love and beauty
See page 50

THESEUS
Founding King of Athens
See page 106

30-SECOND TEXT
Viv Croot

The Minotaur, appeased only by sacrifice, caused terror and dread until it was slain by Theseus.

MEDUSA & THE GORGONS

the 30-second mythology

Medusa's story began when

she slept with Poseidon in a 'forbidden' place, which was either a temple of Athena or a flower meadow – a place where seduction frequently took place in mythology. For this sexual transgression, Athena turned Medusa from a beautiful-haired, young woman into a serpent-haired monster with boar's tusks, a beard, a protruding tongue, wings and a gaze so horrible that it could turn onlookers to stone. But Athena's wrath did not end with this metamorphosis. When Perseus accepted the quest for the head of the Gorgon, Athena helped him decapitate the sleeping monster. Medusa, who was mortal, had two immortal sisters, who shared her monstrous appearance. These were Steno ('mighty') and Euryale ('far-leaping'). Along with Medusa ('cunning'), these daughters of the primordial sea gods, Phorcys and Ceto, were depicted as dwelling at the extreme end of the world, beside the streams of Ocean.

3-SECOND MUSE
Medusa was originally a beautiful woman who was transformed into one of the three Gorgons – the ugliest and most terrifying monsters of the classical world.

3-MINUTE ODYSSEY
Perseus was not just Medusa's slayer but her midwife as well. All the time she was a monster, she was pregnant with her children by Poseidon. These children – the warrior Chrysoar and the winged horse Pegasus – could not be released until Perseus had cut off her head. After various adventures with the head, Perseus presented it to Athena, who put it on her aegis.

RELATED MYTH
The lolling tongue in descriptions of the Hindu goddess Kali is like the protruding tongue of the Gorgons.

3-SECOND BIOGRAPHIES
POSEIDON/NEPTUNE
God of the sea and horses, brother to Zeus
See page 36

ATHENA/MINERVA
Goddess of wisdom, warfare and justice
See page 52

PERSEUS
Greek hero who killed Medusa
See page 108

30-SECOND TEXT
Susan Deacy

Once a beautiful woman, Medusa offends the goddess Athena, who turns her into a hideous, snake-headed Gorgon.

CERBERUS

the 30-second mythology

Cerberus had an impressive pedigree. He was the offspring of two of the most feared monsters in myth, Echidna and Typhon, and was the brother of the Hydra and the Sphinx. Cerberus was one of the hybrids loved by ancient artists, a huge dog with many heads, usually portrayed as three but sometimes as many as fifty. All the heads were wrapped up in a mane of living snakes. As guard dog of the underworld, Cerberus preserved the boundary between life and death, resisting the efforts of heroes who tried to enter the underworld while still alive. Despite his ferocity, Cerberus could be defeated, albeit only temporarily. Orpheus sang him to sleep when he tried to bring back Eurydice, and both Aeneas and Theseus drugged Cerberus with cake. Unfortunately for Theseus, the drug wore off before he could get back out, and he was trapped until Heracles rescued him. Heracles' approach was more direct. He simply overpowered Cerberus, wrestling him to the ground. As the capture of Cerberus was one of the labours set by Eurystheus, Heracles took him to Mycenae, but Eurystheus was so terrified that he hid in a large pot and ordered Heracles to return Cerberus to Hades.

3-SECOND MUSE
Cerberus, a monstrous dog with many heads, guarded the entrance to the underworld, keeping the dead from the living and also the living from the dead.

3-MINUTE ODYSSEY
Snakes symbolized the relationship between life and death. Medusa had snakes for hair, the Chimaera had a snake's tail, Echidna was half woman and half snake, and many figures died from snake bites, including Orpheus' wife, Eurydice.

RELATED MYTH
Where Cerberus keeps people from escaping from Hades, the snake in the Garden of Eden myth (Genesis 3) causes the eviction of the original humans from paradise.

3-SECOND BIOGRAPHIES
HADES
Name given both to the underworld and to its king
See page 82

HERACLES/HERCULES
Son of Alcmene and Zeus, became a god after death
See page 96

THESEUS
Founding King of Athens
See page 106

ORPHEUS
Tried to guide his wife Eurydice back from Hades
See page 120

30-SECOND TEXT
Emma Griffiths

The many-headed guardian of the underworld, Cerberus is a frequent foe of Greek heroes.

POLYPHEMUS & THE CYCLOPES

the 30-second mythology

Returning from Troy, Odysseus

and his companions came to an unknown land. They made their way to a cave, and presently a Cyclops returned with his flocks, closing the mouth of the cave with a great boulder. When the Cyclops, Polyphemus, asked the strangers who they were, Odysseus explained that they were Greeks on their way home from Troy. Polyphemus responded by seizing a couple of the men and devouring them. The Greeks felt helpless, for even if they could kill the giant, they could not push aside the rock that blocked the mouth of the cave. The next morning Polyphemus ate another couple of men. In the evening the giant asked Odysseus his name and Odysseus said he was called 'Nobody'. After the Cyclops fell asleep, the men poked out his eye with a great pointed stake, and Polyphemus awoke, crying out to the other Cyclopes for help, saying that Nobody had injured him. The other Cyclopes assumed he had gone mad. In the morning Polyphemus let his animals out to pasture, feeling among them to make sure the Greeks did not try to escape with them. To avoid detection, however, the Greeks had attached themselves to the undersides of the sheep and slipped out along with the flock.

3-SECOND MUSE
Polyphemus, one of the single-eyed giants known collectively as Cyclopes, was a son of the Greek god Poseidon and the sea nymph Thoosa.

3-MINUTE ODYSSEY
There were two different groups of Cyclopes in Greek mythology, apparently unrelated to each other. One set were blacksmiths who forged thunderbolts for Zeus. They consisted of three brothers, sons of Gaia (earth) and Uranus (sky). The other set were the cannibalistic shepherds whom Odysseus encountered on his way home from Troy. Both groups of Cyclopes were giants with a single eye in the middle of their foreheads.

RELATED MYTH
Polyphemus plays the role of the 'stupid ogre', or slow-witted adversary, who is outwitted by the protagonist. An example of a stupid ogre in Nordic myth is the giant Thrym, who is tricked by the god Thor.

3-SECOND BIOGRAPHIES
THE MINOTAUR
Monstrous being who was part human and part bull
See page 62

MEDUSA & THE GORGONS
Monstrous female beings with snakes for hair
See page 64

CERBERUS
Multi-headed dog of Hades
See page 66

30-SECOND TEXT
William Hansen

Polyphemus' brute strength proves no match for the cunning of Odysseus.

20 March, 43 BC
Born Sulmona, Italy

29–25 BC
Took up poetry full time

25 BC
His first recitation

19 BC
Composed *Heroides*
(*The Heroines*)

16–15 BC
Composed *Amores*
(*The Loves*)

8–3 BC
Second edition of *Amores*

AD 2
Composed *Ars Amatoria*
(*The Art of Love*) and
Remedia Amoris (*The
Cure for Love*)

AD 8
Composed
Metamorphoses; began
work on *Fasti*

AD 8
Exiled to Tomis (modern
Constanta, Romania)

AD 9–12
Composed *Tristia*

AD 17/18
Died in exile

2004
Metamorphoses
translated by David
Raeburn

OVID

Ovid (Publius Ovidius Naso) is one of the best-loved Roman poets. He was immensely popular in his own time, and much imitated by medieval writers.

One of his most popular works, still read today and a source for much of what we know about classical mythology, is the mock-epic *Metamorphoses*, which gives Ovid's original take on 250 myths. The theme of this work is that everything in the cosmos is transitory. There is no one main figure in the work, and even the roughly chronological order is often ignored. The key metamorphosis is of gods acting like, and so almost becoming, humans at the beginning of the work and of humans becoming gods at the end. In between are almost invariably unhappy relations, spurred by love or the failure of it, between gods and humans on the one hand and between humans and humans on the other.

We know a good deal about Ovid because he tells us a lot about himself. Trained as a lawyer, he turned to poetry when he was about 19. A friend of Horace and on distant nodding terms with Virgil, Ovid became the master of the elegiac couplet (a form of lyric poetry). His first major work, *Heroides* (*The Heroines*), was a collection of fictional love letters from mythical heroines to their feckless, absent or absconding lovers. There followed *Amores* (*The Loves*), a series of amorous epistles to a fictional lover, Corinna, but his true blockbuster was undoubtedly *Ars Amatoria* (*The Art of Love*), a three-volume guide to love, seduction and sex for both genders. Ovid then wrote the sequel *Remedia Amoris* (*The Cure for Love*). Also extant is a fragment of *Medicamina Faciei Feminae* (*Treatments for Women's Faces*), probably the first book of beauty tips for women.

Metamorphoses was completed in AD 8, just before Ovid was exiled to the Black Sea by Augustus. Perhaps he was exiled because of his enthusiasm for adultery at a time when Rome was encouraging monogamy, or perhaps his exile was for political reasons. Sadly, he died in exile, leaving unfinished his magnum opus, *Fasti* (*The Festivals*) – an expression of Augustan ideals based on the Roman calendar.

THE HARPIES

the 30-second mythology

The Harpies' first appearance in Greek literature is incongruously charming. For Hesiod, they are goddesses of the scudding storm clouds, 'lovely-haired', keeping pace 'on their swift wings with the blasts of the winds and the birds'. Later the nastier implications of their name 'Snatchers' take over. The classical Harpies are monsters, birds with women's faces, with filthy tempers and filthier habits, shrieking voices and rapacious claws that snatch and carry off anything or anyone. As 'hounds of Zeus', they were sent to torment the blind prophet, King Phineus, who had revealed too many of Zeus' secrets, by snatching away the food from his hands and covering his remaining food with foul droppings. Jason's Argonauts came to the starving king's rescue, and the two winged sons of the North Wind chased the Harpies away to the Strophades islands. There they later confronted Aeneas and his followers with taunting prophecies of starvation. As an emblem of grasping greed and shrill malice, the description 'harpy' has been applied to politicians, lawyers and tax collectors, but it is now almost always a sexist put-down for an insufficiently self-effacing woman.

3-SECOND MUSE
The Harpies – their name means 'Snatchers' – are demonic bird-women. They are emblems of cruelty and rapacity, and are personifications of storm winds.

3-MINUTE ODYSSEY
Virgil places the Harpies at the gate of the underworld, and in Dante's *Inferno* they haunt the Wood of the Suicides, maliciously tearing at the bark and leaves of the suicidal souls who have been transformed into trees. They make a memorable modern appearance in Philip Pullman's *His Dark Materials: The Amber Spyglass* as warders of the land of the dead, cruel and taunting but hungry for true stories of the world above.

RELATED MYTH
The Harpies, while uniquely Greek, are like Celtic goddesses of war and death, who often appeared in the form of predatory ravens or crows.

3-SECOND BIOGRAPHIES
ZEUS/JUPITER
King of Olympus, god of the sky
See page 32

AENEAS
Trojan hero and ancestor of the Romans
See page 104

JASON & MEDEA
Questing hero, leader of the Argonauts, and his wife
See page 122

30-SECOND TEXT
Geoffrey Miles

Monstrous birds with women's heads, the Harpies are the vicious, malicious 'hounds of Zeus'.

THE ERINYES

the 30-second mythology

The Erinyes were deities of

vengeance, who in some versions of myth were born out of the blood that fell to the earth (Gaia) when Cronus castrated his father, Uranus. Other stories make them the children of Nyx, goddess of the night. The Greeks considered them numerous. The Romans, who called them the Furies, assumed just three, who were named Alecto, Tisiphone and Megaera. They punished mortals who committed the unnatural act of killing a blood relative, and represented the horror of kin-killing. Born as old women with claws instead of hands and with snakes instead of hair, they hunted offenders like animals and drove them mad with binding incantations. Their most famous victims were Alcmaeon and Orestes, who had committed matricide to avenge their fathers. In his play *The Eumenides* Aeschylus presents them as pursuing Orestes until Athena pacifies them and replaces their regime of vengeance with a legal system of justice. The Erinyes could also be called upon by a parent's curse to punish a child. Amyntor cursed his son Phoenix for sleeping with his mistress, Althaia cursed her son Meleager after he killed her brothers, and Oedipus is said to have cursed his sons when they imprisoned him after his incest and parricide were revealed.

3-SECOND MUSE
The Erinyes, known to the Romans as the Furies, were deities who punished family bloodshed. They were sometimes referred to euphemistically as 'Eumenides' meaning 'Kindly Ones'.

3-MINUTE ODYSSEY
The Erinyes were unforgiving avengers, who punished blood guilt regardless of the circumstances, seeing all situations in black and white. Similar ideas about the inevitable consequences of actions were personified as Dike ('justice') and Nemesis ('retribution'). Even accidental crimes such as walking on sacred ground would incur an automatic penalty. We are told, perhaps apocryphally, that the appearance of the Furies on stage was so frightening that children fainted and women suffered miscarriages.

RELATED MYTH
The Erinyes were like the Gorgons, three sisters with snakes for hair who turned to stone any person who saw them.

3-SECOND BIOGRAPHIES
URANUS
Sky father to Gaia's earth mother
See page 22

DELPHI
Home to the Delphic Oracle
See page 90

AESCHYLUS
Fifth-century Athenian tragic playwright
See page 100

OEDIPUS
King of Thebes who killed his father and married his mother
See page 116

30-SECOND TEXT
Emma Griffiths

Known to the Romans as the Furies, these sisters exact vengeance for, above all, either parricide or matricide.

GEOGRAPHY

Achaeans People who lived in the north Peloponnesian region of Achaea during the Mycenaean period. The term is used by Homer to refer to the various groups that made up the collective Greek force that besieged Troy. The Achaean League was a confederacy of twelve city-states from the region.

ambrosia Term used to describe the food of the Olympian gods. In most but not all cases, ambrosia is what the gods ate, while nectar is what they drank. The gods would often feed ambrosia to their horses, and Athena gave Heracles ambrosia when he became immortal. The King of Phrygia, Tantalus, having been invited to eat with the gods, was banished to Tartarus for, among other things, attempting to steal ambrosia to give to his human subjects.

cosmos From the Greek word *kosmos* (literally 'order' or 'beauty'). In ancient Greek cosmogony, the cosmos emerged out of the vast emptiness of Chaos, the primordial state of matter. In contrast to the Bible, in which God creates the world by himself but not out of himself, the Greek view of creation, found above all in Hesiod's *Theogony*, is that the emergence of gods is identical with the creation of the world.

Muses Goddesses who inspired creativity in music, dance, literature, art and science and from which are derived the words music, museum and mosaic. To inspire meant to infuse with creativity but not to impart the content, as in revelation. There are usually considered to be nine muses, each of whom is sometimes given responsibility for a specific art. For Hesiod, the muses were the daughters of Zeus and Mnemosyne the goddess associated with memory. In other versions they are depicted as the early, primordial offspring of Gaia and Uranus.

nectar The liquid sustenance of the gods of Olympus.

prophecies Predictions delivered through oracles, such as those at Dodona and Delphi. Much store was set by oracular announcements despite their often being ambiguous. One of the most notorious examples of ambiguous prophecy involved a young Oedipus, who was informed that if he returned home, he would kill his father and sleep with his mother. The home that Oedipus assumed was being referred to was his present home, Corinth. To avoid the dread prophecy he set off for Thebes, the place of his birth – and the rest is history. Prophecies also came in dreams. While accepted as true, prophecies, it was believed, could also be averted – as the case of Oedipus and his father, Laius, illustrated. They were wrong.

psychopomp Name given to an entity that guides newly deceased souls to the afterlife. Psychopomps are found in many religions. Classical examples are Charon, Hermes, Hecate and Morpheus.

Trojan Horse The giant wooden horse in which thirty Greek soldiers, including Odysseus, gained access to Troy. Under the orders of Odysseus, the Greeks constructed the giant horse ostensibly to honour the goddess Athena, whose temple they had destroyed during the war, and thereby to ensure safe passage back to Greece. The Greek fleet then appeared to set sail home. The Trojans, tricked by Sinon, dragged the horse into the city and proceeded to celebrate the Greeks' departure. Sinon later opened the horse to let out the soldiers, who then opened the city gates to admit the returning Greek forces and bring about the sacking of Troy.

MOUNT OLYMPUS

the 30-second mythology

3-SECOND MUSE
Mount Olympus was
the mountain of the
gods, where they lived
in a beautiful palace in
endless feasting under
the watchful Zeus.

3-MINUTE ODYSSEY
Otus ('doom') and
Ephialtes ('nightmare')
were sons of Poseidon.
The brothers decided to
attack Mount Olympus.
To get high enough, they
piled Mount Ossa and
Mount Pelion, other
mountains of Thessaly,
on top of one another.
Artemis jumped between
them in the form of a deer.
Casting their spears, they
missed and instead struck
each other dead.

At 2917 metres (9570 feet),

Mount Olympus is the tallest mountain in
Greece and one of the highest peaks in Europe.
It is part of the range that separates the plain
of Macedonia from Thessaly. No ancient Greek
ever climbed it, as far as we know, and in the
poetic imagination it was the home of the gods.
There, high above the clouds, the Olympians
had their palace, except for Poseidon and
Hades, who dwelled in the sea and in the
underworld. The gods spent their time dining
on ambrosia, a magical food, and drinking
nectar, a magical drink (both words probably
mean 'deathless'). As they feasted, Apollo sang
and played his lyre, much as the oral poets
entertained at earthly courts, with the Muses
accompanying him in choral song. When the
sun went down, the gods retired to their private
dwellings, built by Hephaestus. Although the
gods on Olympus lived eternally in a divine
paradise, Olympus was very much part of earth
rather than a transcendent, spiritual place.

RELATED MYTH
The biblical Tower of
Babel was an attempt to
reach and thereby equal,
if not overthrow, God.

3-SECOND BIOGRAPHIES
ZEUS/JUPITER
King of Olympus, god
of the sky
See page 32

HERA/JUNO
Queen of the gods, wife
of Zeus/Jupiter
See page 34

HEPHAESTUS/VULCAN
God of crafts, blacksmith
to the gods
See page 38

APOLLO
God of music, prophecy,
and, later, the sun
See page 42

30-SECOND TEXT
Barry B. Powell

*The home of most of
the gods, Olympus is a
paradise of continual
feasting and music.*

HADES

the 30-second mythology

According to Greek mythology, nearly all human beings proceeded after death to a subterranean realm ruled by the dreaded king and queen of the dead, Hades and his wife Persephone. The realm was known as the House of Hades, suggesting a built structure, or simply Hades. Another common name was Erebus (ancient Greek, 'darkness'), which implied a murky region where the souls of the dead roamed. Within Hades there were streams and lakes with names identifying misery, such as Acheron ('grief'), Cocytus ('wailing') and Phlegethon ('burning'). Although the waters of the Styx ('hateful') are widely regarded as separating Hades from the land of the living, it was across the Acheron that the ferryman Charon transported newly deceased souls for a fee. Alternatively, Hermes Psychopompos ('Escorter-of-Souls') led the souls of the dead through the air to their new abode. Once the dead entered through Hades' gate, they were prevented from leaving by Hades' many-headed hell hound, Cerberus. Although the souls resembled their former selves, so that they were recognizable and retained their personalities and memories, they had no more substance than smoke or reflections in water. They could enjoy no sensory pleasures and did not eat, converse or reflect. Instead, they spent eternity inactive in a realm of darkness.

3-SECOND MUSE
In Greek cosmogony (relating to the origin of the universe), Hades was the place where humans resided after death, and also the name of the ruler of the dead.

3-MINUTE ODYSSEY
The House of Hades was not primarily a realm of punishment or reward, but merely the place where humans went when they died, whether they had led moral or immoral lives. Nevertheless, a few souls remained embodied and experienced exceptional treatment, for better or worse. For example, Sisyphus had the never-ending task of rolling a stone up a hill over and over again, while the renowned hunter Orion happily passed his time hunting game.

RELATED MYTH
A realm in which mortals carry on an existence of some kind after death is found in many mythologies. Examples are the House of Yama (India), Sheol (Israel), Niflheim (Scandinavia) and House of Donn (Ireland).

3-SECOND BIOGRAPHIES
CERBERUS
Multi-headed dog of Hades
See page 66

TARTARUS
Cosmic prison for defeated gods and monsters
See page 86

HERACLES/HERCULES
Greek hero of immense strength
See page 96

30-SECOND TEXT
William Hansen

The underground realm is presided over by its namesake, the king of the dead.

480 BC
Born at Salamis, Greece

455 BC
First City Dionysia competition

441 BC
Won first prize at City Dionysia

C. 406 BC
Died in Macedonia

405 BC
The Bacchae and *Iphigenia in Aulis* performed at the City Dionysia, and took first prize

C. AD 200
Ten of Euripides' plays published in text form

1955
Alcestis translated by Richmond Lattimore; *The Medea* translated by Rex Warner; *The Heracleidae* translated by Ralph Gladstone; *Hippolytus* translated by David Grene

EURIPIDES

Following Aeschylus and

Sophocles, Euripides was the last of the three great Greek tragedians, and probably the one most familiar to modern audiences. This is partly because eighteen or so of the possible ninety-two plays he wrote survive intact, with many performances taking place today. His plots are more complex than those of Aeschylus or Sophocles. He marginalizes the chorus far more than either of them did. He develops his characters even more fully than they did. Above all, he 'psychologizes' his characters, ascribing to them realistic, if still lamentable, motives. Of him, it has been commonly said that he writes about humans as they are and not as they ought to be.

In half of his plays Euripides introduces the sudden appearance at the end of a play of a god suspended from a crane – the technique know as *deus ex machina* ('god out of the machine'). The god serves to resolve an otherwise remaining confusion in the play. Ancient literary critics like Aristotle criticized the practice on the grounds that resolution should come from the story itself and not from something external imported into the story.

Scholars debate whether Euripides actually believed in the gods. If not, *deus ex machina* is almost a caricature of standard deference to gods. At the least, Euripides castigates the gods as cruel, capricious and above all irrational. Seen this way, he wants to reform,

not reject, divinity. In his refusal to genuflect before the gods, he breaks with both Aeschylus and Sophocles. At the most, Euripides dismisses as irrational the belief in gods themselves. When he is taken to be going this far, he is translating the gods into projections of human characteristics, which is what Friedrich Nietzsche and Sigmund Freud both did in modern times. Nietzsche himself assumes that Euripides is not an atheist and that his enlistment of a *deus ex machina* is intended to vindicate them as forces of rationality and moderation.

Euripides was the least popular of the three major tragedians. He won only five prizes at the City Dionysia drama festivals, and one of those posthumously. One reason for this might have been his brave and provocative sympathy for women, especially for those mistreated by men. He presents a gallery of powerful, though flawed, heroines. One of his most celebrated heroines is Medea, who saves her husband Jason's life only to be abandoned by him for someone else. Another celebrated heroine is Electra, who abets her brother, Orestes, in the killing of their mother, Clytemnestra. Euripides' unrelenting condemnation of war doubtless also made him unpopular.

We know little about Euripides' personal life other than that he was married twice and allegedly wrote his plays in what is now the Cave of Euripides in Syracuse.

TARTARUS

the 30-second mythology

Tartarus is the lowest of the worlds that make up the cosmos. Hesiod claims that if a bronze anvil should fall from the sky, it would land on the earth ten days later, and if it should fall from the earth, it would likewise reach Tartarus on the tenth day. Tartarus is therefore as far beneath the earth as the earth is beneath the sky. Tartarus serves as a cosmic prison. Gods and monsters can be defeated, but since they are supernatural beings, they are ordinarily not subject to death. What are the ruling gods to do with powerful enemies they have vanquished but cannot kill? They put them in indefinite storage in Tartarus. It is there that the Olympian gods imprisoned their adversaries, the Titans, and it is there that Zeus confined the huge monster Typhon after their combat. Since the prisoners are strong, Tartarus is surrounded by a bronze wall, and since the prisoners are huge, Tartarus is necessarily vast. According to Hesiod, a person entering through its bronze door would be tossed about in the darkness by great winds for a full year before reaching its bottom. Tartarus is also the prison for those human beings who have most insulted or challenged the gods, such as Tantalus and Sisyphus.

3-SECOND MUSE
Tartarus is a vast, underworld prison for defeated gods and monsters, and also for some humans.

3-MINUTE ODYSSEY
Like other parts of the mythic cosmos such as Gaia (Earth), Uranus (Sky) and Hades (land of the dead), Tartarus is at once a place and a personality. As a place, Tartarus is a prison. As a personality, Tartarus is the son of Gaia, with whom he mates.

RELATED MYTH
In many mythic traditions supernatural beings can only be confined and not slain. For example, in Nordic myth the god Loki and the huge wolf Fenrir are fettered by the ruling gods.

3-SECOND BIOGRAPHIES
GAIA
Mother earth
See page 18

URANUS
Father sky
See page 22

HADES
Realm of the dead
See page 82

30-SECOND TEXT
William Hansen

Tartarus is both a personality in his own right and the domain that he controls.

TROY

the 30-second mythology

According to Greek mythology,

Troy was a major trading city on the western coast of modern-day Turkey and the scene of an epic war 'between the Trojans, tamers of horses, and the bronze-clad Achaeans'. The war began when Paris, son of the Trojan King Priam, went in quest of the most beautiful woman in the world, and came back with Helen, wife of the Spartan King Menelaus. In response, Agamemnon, Menelaus' brother, led a thousand Greek ships on a 'shock and awe' expedition against Troy. But like the recent war in Iraq, the siege lasted for many years. Heroes on both sides – Hector, Achilles, Ajax – fought, quarrelled and died beneath Troy's massive walls, and all the while the gods watched and interfered. Eventually, the city, which had resisted force, fell to cunning. The wily Odysseus constructed the original 'Trojan Horse' – a giant wooden trophy that the Trojans triumphantly dragged into their city, unaware that it contained Greek soldiers. Troy fell in flames, Menelaus reclaimed Helen and the Greeks – some of them – returned home. From Homer through Euripides, Virgil, Chaucer and Shakespeare to the 2004 movie *Troy*, the Trojan War has become our most iconic image of the glory, brutality and tragedy of war.

3-SECOND MUSE
Troy was a legendary city besieged for ten years by the Greeks. The Trojan War has become the archetypal war story in Western culture.

3-MINUTE ODYSSEY
While the ancient Greeks assumed that Troy and the Trojan War were real, historians believed that both were made up. Then, in the 1870s, the German archaeologist-adventurer Heinrich Schliemann claimed to have uncovered the ruins of Troy at Hissarlik in Turkey. Excavations on a grand scale continue, and most experts assume that Troy did exist and that a battle involving a siege probably took place; but whether an event on the scale described in the *Iliad* occurred remains questionable.

RELATED MYTH
Legends of similarly epic proportions in other cultures include the Indian *Mahabharata*, the German *Nibelungenlied* and the French *Chanson de Roland*.

3-SECOND BIOGRAPHIES
HOMER
Early Greek epic poet, author of the *Iliad* and *Odyssey*
See page 44

ACHILLES
Greek warrior, hero of the *Iliad*
See page 98

ODYSSEUS/ULYSSES
King of Ithaca and great strategist of the Trojan War
See page 102

AENEAS
Trojan hero, ancestor of the Romans
See page 104

30-SECOND TEXT
Geoffrey Miles

The conquest of Troy is one of the most enduring tales in all of mythology.

DELPHI

the 30-second mythology

Delphi was the belly button of the mythological universe. Zeus conducted an aerial survey using two eagles to find the centre of the world, and the place where the eagles met was marked with a stone called an *omphalos* (Greek for 'navel'). The most famous location for this meeting point was Delphi, a religious centre initially dedicated to the goddesses Gaia, Themis and Phoebe before the site passed to Apollo after he killed the snake Python. Apollo's prophecies were conveyed through the Pythian priestess, who entered a trance, possibly aided by chewing bay leaves. Archaeologists have suggested that the geology of Delphi may have inspired the myth, as hallucinogenic gases rose from the deep chasm in the cliff. On the one hand the oracle in myth could be very specific. For example, Oedipus' father Laius was told that if he had a child, this son would kill his father. On the other hand the oracle was renowned for giving ambiguous meanings. Oedipus, having been told that he was not the son of the King and Queen of Corinth, asked the oracle who his real parents were. He was informed only that he would kill his father and marry his mother. Assuming the oracle was referring to his present Corinthian parents, he immediately fled Corinth for Thebes.

3-SECOND MUSE
Delphi was home of the Delphic Oracle, a sacred site where Apollo delivered prophecies through the voice of the Pythian priestess.

3-MINUTE ODYSSEY
The temple of Apollo at Delphi had two mottoes: 'Nothing in excess' and 'Know thyself'. The ambiguous, oracular advice may reflect the importance of these psychological warnings. A similar warning may be taken from the myth of Cassandra: Apollo gave her the gift of prophecy when she promised to sleep with him. But when she did not, he added a curse that her prophecies would never be believed.

RELATED MYTH
The role of the Castellian spring, used for purification at Delphi, recalls the Norse myth of the prophet Mimir, who protected the sacred well beneath the Tree of the World.

3-SECOND BIOGRAPHIES
ZEUS/JUPITER
King of Olympus, god of the sky
See page 32

APOLLO
God of the sun, music and poetry
See page 42

OEDIPUS
Tragic Greek figure, who killed his father and married his mother
See page 116

30-SECOND TEXT
Emma Griffiths

The centre of the world, Delphi is the spiritual heartland of Apollo and home of the Delphic Oracle.

HEROES ◑

Aeneid Virgil's epic poem, which recounts the story of Aeneas, a Trojan prince, who, after a series of adventures, eventually establishes a settlement in Latium, thereby founding what becomes Rome. Organized into twelve books and written between 29 and 19 BC, the poem borrows from the *Odyssey* and *Iliad*. At the same time it makes reference and pays tribute to the deeds and rule of Virgil's own Emperor Augustus.

centaurs Half-man, half-horse creatures, who exemplify untamed, wild nature. They are often depicted as the lustful, drunken followers of Dionysus. An exception is the centaur Chiron, who is a tutor to various heroes, including Achilles, Ajax, Theseus and, in some versions, Heracles, who was known for his intelligence and not just for his strength. While the centaurs were usually depicted as males, there were occasionally female centaurs.

Elysium (the Elysian Fields) A region of the underworld which, unlike Hades, is the equivalent of heaven. Whereas practically everyone went to Hades – except for those consigned to Tartarus – only a few went to Elysium, which was the final resting place for heroes or those deemed especially dutiful. An example is Aeneas' father, Anchises, who is described by Virgil as living in a realm of perpetual spring. According to one source, Cronus ruled over Elysium. Although Elysium is mentioned in the *Odyssey*, Odysseus never visited. By contrast, Aeneas in Virgil's *Aeneid* went there to confer with his father, Anchises.

Graeae Two or usually three sisters of the Gorgons. They shared a single eye and tooth. They were the daughters of Phorcys and Ceto and, like their parents, were ancient sea goddesses. Usually portrayed as old, grey hags, though sometimes with the bodies of swans, they had their eye and tooth stolen by Perseus, who then forced them to tell him of their Gorgon sisters' whereabouts.

Iliad Homer's epic poem, which recounts a few months during the last year of the Trojan War, although there are many references to prior events. Written in around 800 BC, the poem is arranged into twenty-four books, and deals with the nearly universal themes of fate and free will, divinity and humanity, pride and glory, compassion and love and hate, and life and death. It is one of the most influential works of Western literature.

River Styx Perhaps the best known to modern audiences of the rivers that flow through the underworld realm of Hades. The Styx was said to flow around Hades seven or nine times and to form the boundary between the living and the dead. Considered sacred even by the gods themselves, it was the river in which Thetis dipped her son Achilles when an infant, thereby making his body invincible – apart from the heel by which she held him.

Sirens Three sea nymphs who used an irresistible song to lure sailors to their deaths on the rocks close to the island where they lived. Demeter cursed them with the bodies of birds for failing to prevent her daughter Persephone's abduction by Hades. Jason and his Argonauts avoided disaster when the Sirens sang thanks to Orpheus, whose playing drowned them out. Odysseus ordered his men to block their ears so that they could not hear them, but he had himself tied to the mast so that he could hear but would be able to resist.

Twelve labours The twelve challenges that Heracles had to undertake as punishment for killing his wife and children during a fit of madness caused by his erstwhile enemy Hera. Having recovered his senses and witnessed his crime, Heracles travelled to Delphi to ask the oracle how he could atone. He was told, he must serve under King Eurystheus for twelve years, who set Heracles the labours. Traditionally the labours were: 1) killing the Nemean lion; 2) killing the Lernaean Hydra; 3) capturing the hind of Ceryneia; 4) capturing the Erymanthian boar; 5) cleaning the Augean stables; 6) driving away the Stymphalian birds; 7) capturing the Cretan bull; 8) stealing the man-eating horses of Diomedes; 9) stealing the belt of the Hippolyte; 10) capturing the cattle of Geryon; 11) stealing the apples of the Hesperides; and 12) capturing Cerberus.

HERACLES/ HERCULES

the 30-second mythology

As the 'Glory of Hera', which is

what 'Heracles' means, the hero was linked by name to Hera, the greatest of his persecutors. Humiliated by her husband Zeus' escapade with another woman, she worked against Heracles even before his birth. She secured for Eurystheus, his mortal victimizer, the kingship that Zeus had intended for Heracles. When Hera put serpents in Heracles' cot to kill him, he killed them instead, demonstrating the strength that would later get him through his various exploits, not least the twelve labours. These labours took him from his Peloponnesian homeland to exotic locations, and even to the edge of the earth and the underworld. Heracles died, effectively, at the hands of one of his long dead victims: the centaur Nessus, whom he had killed while Nessus was trying to rape his wife, Deianira. Believing it to be a love potion, Deianira gave Heracles a robe soaked in Nessus' blood; as its poison was eating into his flesh, Heracles insisted upon being thrown upon his funeral pyre. After he died, Athena conveyed him by chariot to Mount Olympus. The marriage of Heracles to Hebe symbolized his divine rebirth while also marking his reconciliation with Hebe's mother, his erstwhile enemy Hera.

3-SECOND MUSE
Heracles, known in Rome as Hercules, was the son of Zeus and Alcmena. The most celebrated of the classical heroes, he transcended mortality and joined the Olympian gods.

3-MINUTE ODYSSEY
Heracles was noted not only for his extraordinary feats of strength and endurance, but also for his intelligence, skills and musicianship. Among his traits were an excessive temper, a sexual prowess that once saw him deflower 50 maidens in a single night, and a tendency towards spells of madness that produced atrocities, the worst of which was the killing of his children and his first wife Megara. His accepted punishment was his twelve labours.

RELATED MYTH
Heracles was regarded in antiquity as comparable with Melqart, the 'Thasian Heracles' (Herodotus 2.44). There are also parallels with the biblical figures Samson and Goliath.

3-SECOND BIOGRAPHIES
ZEUS/JUPITER
King of Olympus, god of the sky
See page 32

HERA/JUNO
Queen of the gods, wife of Zeus/Jupiter
See page 34

30-SECOND TEXT
Susan Deacy

The greatest of the heroes, Heracles is best known for his twelve labours. The first was wrestling a famous lion and the last was bringing the hell hound Cerberus to the surface of the earth.

αβγδεϛξηθια

ACHILLES

the 30-second mythology

Achilles was the son of Peleus, the mortal King of the Myrmidons, and Thetis, a nymph, who tried to make the baby Achilles immortal by dipping him in the River Styx. Unfortunately, she overlooked the spot on his heel by which she held him in the river, thereby leaving him vulnerable to a mortal injury in that place. Achilles was given a choice by the gods: either to have a short life filled with glory or to have a long life lived in obscurity. He chose the first option and became the greatest Greek warrior in the Trojan War. Homer's epic poem the *Iliad* tells of Achilles' anger when he was insulted by King Agamemnon, who took away a slave woman given to him as a battle prize. Achilles refused to fight. But when the Greeks began to suffer losses, his friend Patroclus begged to borrow his armour and fight. Patroclus fought well but was killed by Achilles' Trojan counterpart, Hector. In a rage Achilles not only killed Hector but also defiled his body and relented only when Hector's father, Priam, came to beg for its return. Near the end of the Trojan War Achilles died when he was struck on the heel by an arrow fired by another Trojan prince, Paris.

3-SECOND MUSE
The greatest fighter of the Trojan War, he chose a short life of glory over a long life in obscurity.

3-MINUTE ODYSSEY
In some versions of the myth, Achilles was transported to Elysium and married Medea, but in Homer's *Odyssey* the shade of Achilles appears to Odysseus and regrets his decision to die young and spend eternity in Hades. Although he is consoled when he hears from the visiting Odysseus about his son, Neoptolemos, his continuing sadness undermines the traditional epic insistence on the value of glory.

RELATED MYTH
The idea of a hero made invulnerable but for a single missed spot is also seen in the Teutonic story of Siegfried and the Indian story of Krishna.

3-SECOND BIOGRAPHIES
TROY
Legendary city-state and the location of the Trojan War
See page 88

ODYSSEUS/ULYSSES
King of Ithaca and great strategist of the Trojan War
See page 102

30-SECOND TEXT
Emma Griffiths

Achilles' superhuman skill as a fighter was compromised by his self-centredness. Today, the 'Achilles' heel' is a metaphor for a character flaw or imperfection in even the most celebrated mortal.

c. 525/4 BC
Born at Eleusis, Greece

499 BC
First performance of
a work

490 BC
Fought at Battle of
Marathon

484 BC
First victory at City
Dionysia

480 BC
Fought at Battle of
Salamis

472 BC
First production of *The
Persians* staged

472 BC
Staged four plays,
financed by Pericles

467 BC
First production of the
Seven Against Thebes

464 BC
First production of *The
Suppliants*

458 BC
First production of *The
Oresteia* staged

c. 445/6 BC
Died at Syracuse, Sicily

1953
The Oresteia translated
by Richmond Lattimore

1977
The Oresteia translated
by Robert Fagles

AESCHYLUS

Aeschylus was the father of classical tragedy. His most celebrated successors, Sophocles and Euripides, made significant changes to the genre, but they built on his achievements. To be sure, Aeschylus himself inherited tragedy of a kind, but he transformed the genre by introducing a second actor, thereby increasing the dialogue and also making the chorus less important. He made the conventional trilogy into a unified set of plays. Previously, playwrights composed three separate plays plus a bawdy satyr play. Of Aeschylus' trilogies, only *The Oresteia* remains.

Thematically, Aeschylus' plays, of which only six or seven out of seventy or so survive, focus on human responsibility for actions. Aeschylus deems the standard appeal to Fate or to the gods an evasion of responsibility. At the same time he advocates devotion to the gods, to whom humans must submit, and sees them as more good than evil. He traces the development of the gods from wrathful forces into figures of mercy as well as justice. He berates gods as well as humans for excessive pride and espouses moderation. He believes that from suffering, which his characters invariably endure, can come wisdom.

Aeschylus' first play, *The Persians*, is about the Battle of Salamis and was unique in Greek tragedy in dealing with contemporary events. In *Seven Against Thebes* he blames humans themselves for parricide and incest rather than attributing them to a divine curse, which was the common explanation. His *Oresteia* tells the story of the life of King Agamemnon of Argos and of the destruction of him and his family. It is also the only complete extant trilogy of any classical Greek playwright.

Aeschylus was born at Eleusis, northwest of Athens. This city was famous for its cult of Demeter. Although an initiate into the cult of Demeter, he was inspired even more by Dionysus. Greek drama began in the Dionysia, which were festivals held in honour of the god. Aeschylus' work was very successful in its time – he won at the City Dionysia competitions thirteen times – and is still widely performed today.

Yet Aeschylus was also a soldier. He fought at both Marathon and Salamis, defending Greece from the invading Persians. His epitaph ignores his contribution to the dramatic arts and concentrates on his military prowess.

ODYSSEUS/ULYSSES
the 30-second mythology

Perhaps the most famous example of Odysseus' cunning, for which he was most celebrated, was the scheme he devised to end the siege of Troy. The Trojan Horse, in which he hid Greek warriors, has become a symbol for deception. However, Odysseus' cunning was not limited to Troy and to his many adventures en route home. Earlier, while on Ithaca, he had attempted to avoid joining Agamemnon's army by pretending to be mad. Yet for all his cunning, Odysseus was capable of moments of arrogance, as when, in sailing away from the island of the Cyclopes, he revealed his actual name to Polyphemus, the Cyclops he had just deceived. This disclosure brought upon him the wrath of Poseidon, Polyphemus' father, who, as the god of the sea, was well placed to impede Odysseus' journey home. Among the various females who doted upon Odysseus was the Phaeacian girl Nausicaa, who encouraged her people to become so well disposed to him when he was shipwrecked on their island that they provided him with ships for his voyage back to Ithaca. With Athena, meanwhile, he concocted the plot to defeat the suitors who had been occupying his place and courting his wife.

3-SECOND MUSE
Odysseus, known as Ulysses in Latin, was the hero whose cleverness enabled him to overcome what for anyone else would have been insurmountable obstacles to his return from the Trojan War.

3-MINUTE ODYSSEY
Odysseus' travels en route home took him as far as the edge of the ocean, where he encountered the shades of the dead. The living characters he met on his journey home included the enchantress Circe; the sweet-singing Sirens, whom Odysseus alone heard and lived to tell about; and the goddess Calypso, who kept him marooned for seven years as her beloved.

RELATED MYTH
Among the heroes whose adventures parallel Odysseus' are Aeneas and Sinbad the Sailor.

3-SECOND BIOGRAPHIES
POSEIDON/NEPTUNE
God of the sea and horses, brother to Zeus
See page 36

ATHENA/MINERVA
Goddess of wisdom, warfare and justice
See page 52

POLYPHEMUS
The Cyclops son of Poseidon
See page 68

30-SECOND TEXT
Susan Deacy

Odysseus was so thoroughly distinguished for his unchecked scheming that he shared the epithet polymetis ('cunning in many ways') with his divine helper, Athena.

AENEAS

the 30-second mythology

A secondary character in the *Iliad*, Aeneas is the main character in Virgil's Roman epic, the *Aeneid*. When Troy fell to the Greeks, Aeneas escaped, carrying his old father on his back and the images of the gods in his hands, with orders from Jupiter (Zeus) himself to lead the Trojan survivors to a new homeland and a historic destiny. Much like Odysseus, Aeneas wandered for years, storm tossed, chasing elusive prophecies. In Carthage, Aeneas and Queen Dido fell in love, but the gods said 'move on!' and Dido killed herself. When he finally reached Italy, Aeneas was embroiled in another war against the local resistance leader, Turnus. At last he was able to found his new city, the precursor of Rome, though he did not live to enjoy it. Aeneas was a new kind of Roman hero, different from glorious Achilles or tricky Odysseus. Virgil's word for him is *pius* – self-denyingly driven by *pietas*, or duty to gods, family and nation. He received from the gods a shield on which was engraved the future history of Rome, and 'he takes up on his shoulder the destined fame of his descendants'. He is a reluctant hero who must literally shoulder the burden of history. In death the gods made him immortal.

3-SECOND MUSE
'Arms and the man I sing.' The man was Aeneas, a Trojan prince, the human son of Venus (Aphrodite), destined to become the ancestor of the Romans.

3-MINUTE ODYSSEY
It took some creative handling of myth and history for Virgil, or his sources, to link the fall of Troy (twelfth century BC) to the founding of Rome (traditionally 753 BC); three centuries of kings had to be invented to bridge the gap from Aeneas to Romulus. An impossible love affair between Aeneas and Dido, founder of Carthage (eighth century BC), supplied a mythic origin for the Punic Wars.

RELATED MYTH
Aeneas bears some likeness to the biblical Moses, another hero commanded by God to lead his followers in long wandering but who dies before entering the Promised Land.

3-SECOND BIOGRAPHIES
ZEUS/JUPITER
King of Olympus, god of the sky
See page 32

APHRODITE/VENUS
Goddess of love and beauty
See page 50

DIDO
Queen of Carthage, Aeneas' tragic lover
See page 126

VIRGIL
Roman epic poet, author of the *Aeneid*
See page 128

30-SECOND TEXT
Geoffrey Miles

Driven by duty, Aeneas was a new, Roman breed of hero.

THESEUS

the 30-second mythology

3-SECOND MUSE
Theseus was a culture
hero, who helped civilize
the world by ridding it of
beasts. He was also hailed
as a reformer for
establishing the political
system of Athens.

3-MINUTE ODYSSEY
Theseus was the product
of a liaison on Sphairia
between his mother, the
Troezenian princess
Aethra, and either the
Athenian King Aegeas or
the god Poseidon. He was
born as a result of trickery,
although the deceiver's
identity varies, as does
that of the victim. Either
Pittheus, Aethra's father,
made Aegeas drunk before
getting him to sleep with
Aethra, or Athena told
Aethra to go to Sphairia,
where, caught off guard,
Poseidon slept with her.

When he reached manhood
and lifted the boulder covering the sword
and sandals of his father, Aegeus, Theseus
demonstrated the strength that marked him
as a hero in the mould of Heracles. Travelling
to Athens to claim his birthright, he chose the
overland route rather than the short sea
crossing in order to slay the various brigands,
rulers and monsters that victimized the localities
along the way. Having reached Athens, and
having overcome his stepmother Medea's
attempts to kill him, he managed to rid the city
of its obligation to Minos. He sailed to Crete
with a group of youths sent as offerings to the
Minotaur but then killed the creature, aided by
Ariadne, daughter of Minos. She escaped with
him only to be abandoned on Naxos. When
Theseus forgot to replace the black sail that
would denote failure with a white one, Aegeus,
thinking his son was dead, threw himself
into the sea, which bore his name thereafter.
Theseus' other adventures included an
expedition to Amazonland and a failed attempt
to abduct Persephone that left his accomplice,
Perithous, stuck forever in Hades. Theseus'
life ended when, like his father, he fell off a
cliff, in his case pushed by Lycomedes.

RELATED MYTH
The theme of travelling to
a distant land, defeating a
monster, and escaping with
the local maiden who assists
is consistent with a
widespread folktale motif
of the 'helper-maiden'.

3-SECOND BIOGRAPHIES
POSEIDON/NEPTUNE
God of the sea and horses,
brother to Zeus
See page 36

THE MINOTAUR
Monstrous being – part man,
part bull
See page 62

HERACLES/HERCULES
Greek hero of immense
strength
See page 96

30-SECOND TEXT
Susan Deacy

*Like many other
classical heroes,
Theseus had a life
that was both
glorious and tragic.*

PERSEUS

the 30-second mythology

Perseus' birth exemplified his

father's ability to beget children in unusual guises, this time as the golden shower that infiltrated the tower in which Danaë was imprisoned. The reason for the imprisonment was a warning from an oracle received by Danaë's father, Acrisius, that her son would kill him. On discovering that Danaë had, despite his actions, borne a child, Acrisius cast the pair adrift in a chest. Some years later, Perseus travelled from Seriphos, the island where the chest had washed ashore and where he had then been raised by a fisherman whose brother was Polydectes, king of the island. Polydectes wanted Perseus out of the way so that he could marry Danaë, Perseus' mother. But Perseus succeeded in the deed that Polydectes had assumed would get him killed: beheading Medusa, the sole Gorgon who was mortal. He was helped by Athena and Hermes as well as by a triad of unwilling helpers, the Graeae, who were the sisters of the Gorgons. Further assistance came from the nymphs, who, according to some accounts, furnished him with four aids: the cap of invisibility normally worn by Hades, a pair of winged sandals that enabled him to fly to 'Gorgonland' and later escape from Medusa's surviving sisters, an adamantine sickle to cut off Medusa's head and a bag in which to store the head.

RELATED MYTH
A hero encountering three elderly persons, who are often women and who sometimes share a single eye, is a folkloristic motif found in other cultures.

3-SECOND BIOGRAPHIES
ZEUS/JUPITER
King of Olympus, god of the sky
See page 32

ATHENA/MINERVA
Goddess of wisdom, warfare and justice
See page 52

HERMES/MERCURY
Messenger of the gods
See page 54

MEDUSA AND THE GORGONS
Serpent-haired monsters
See page 64

30-SECOND TEXT
Susan Deacy

The product of one of Zeus' many illicit affairs, Perseus famously beheads the Gorgon Medusa.

TRAGIC FIGURES

TRAGIC FIGURES
GLOSSARY

Argonauts Named after the ship in which they sailed, the *Argo*, the Argonauts were a group of heroic adventurers who joined Jason on his voyage to Colchis (modern Georgia) in search of the Golden Fleece. Their number varies from source to source, but most accounts suggest there were around fifty. Often included among them were Heracles, Orpheus and Theseus. Ancient Greeks often claimed descent from the named Argonauts.

Golden Fleece The fleece of a golden, winged ram that was required by Jason in order for him to accede to the throne of Iolcus. Many years earlier, the ram had been sent by Hermes to save the lives of a king's son and daughter, whose jealous stepmother had plotted to kill them. The ram carried them off on its back, but the daughter, Helle, fell into the sea (hence Hellespont) before reaching the safety of Colchis (modern Georgia). The son sacrificed the ram to Zeus, and its fleece was placed in an oak tree. Jason's quest for the fleece was instigated by the duplicitous King of Iolcus, Pelias, who expected the quest to lead to Jason's death.

Maenads ('mad ones') Female followers of Dionysus, the god of wine and ecstasy. Under the influence of alcohol, the Maenads would perform orgiastic rituals, which often involved tearing animals apart. They were said to have killed Pentheus and Orpheus, both of whom had failed to honour Dionysus.

metamorphosis The transformation of one object into another. In mythology the change is usually of a human into an animal or plant. Ancient Greek mythology is full of examples of metamorphoses, often either undertaken deliberately by a god or goddess in order to fulfil a personal quest or ambition, such as Zeus turning himself into a swan in order to seduce Leda, or enacted on a mortal by a god or goddess as a form of punishment, such as when Artemis turned Actaeon into a stag. It has long been suggested that the stories of metamorphoses in early religions explain the reverse transformation: from animal worship to the worship of more humanlike deities.

Orphic Mysteries A collection of sacred verses attributed to the mythological figure Orpheus, in whose name was established the cult of Orphism. Adherents of Orphism believed in the dual nature of mankind – part divine (inherited from Dionysus) and part evil (inherited from the Titans). Only by following a strict ethical path and ascetic practices could the divine win over the evil.

Seven Against Thebes The seven champions of the Argive army that led attacks on the seven gates of the Egyptian city of Thebes. Following Oedipus' self-imposed exile from Thebes, it was agreed that his sons Eteocles and Polyneices would rule alternately. However, after the first year Eteocles refused to cede the throne to his brother. In response, Polyneices gathered an army from Argos and attacked Thebes. During the ensuing battle the brothers killed each other, and the Argive army was defeated. A family already suffering from incest and patricide now endured fratricide.

Sphinx In Greek mythology, the Sphinx was a female monster, thought by some to be the offspring of Echidna and Typhon, with a woman's head, a lion's body and an eagle's wings. She was sent to Thebes (by Hera according to some) to avenge a past wrong-doing. She posed a riddle given to her by the Muses, and with each wrong answer a Theban was devoured. Oedipus answered the riddle correctly, and the Sphinx threw herself off a cliff and died. As reward, Oedipus was crowned King of Thebes and then married the newly widowed queen, his mother.

ADONIS

the 30-second mythology

Adonis represented the cycle of nature: life-death-rebirth. The myths surrounding his role as lover of Aphrodite stress his great beauty and his tragic early death. Details of his parentage and birth vary, but a popular version tells how he was born after Aphrodite cursed his mother, often called Smyrna (Roman 'Myrrha'), with an unnatural sexual desire for her own father. When Smyrna's father discovered his unwitting incest, he tried to kill his daughter, but the gods took pity and turned her into a tree, from which Adonis was born. Aphrodite was dazzled by the beauty of the 'babe' and for protection placed him in a chest, which she asked Persephone to guard. When Persephone could not resist opening the chest and saw the child, she in turn wished to keep him for herself. Zeus adjudicated their dispute, allowing Adonis to live for four months with each goddess and four months with whomever he wished. Adonis chose Aphrodite. As a young man, Adonis remained a favourite of Aphrodite. Cosseted and naive to the dangers of hunting, he was killed by a boar, possibly sent by a jealous Ares, but was allowed to return to life for six months of each year to spend with Aphrodite.

3-SECOND MUSE
Adonis was a beautiful young man, beloved of Aphrodite and was associated with fertility.

3-MINUTE ODYSSEY
Mortal men loved by goddesses often came to unfortunate ends. Calypso despaired when Hermes, sent by Zeus, ordered her to free Odysseus, though he came to a happy end. Aurora obtained immortality for her lover Tithonus but forgot to ask for eternal youth, so that he grew old while she stayed young. In *The Golden Bough*, James Frazer turns the human Adonis into a god (of vegetation), and portrays him as an example of the myth of the dying and rising god.

RELATED MYTH
Zeus' acting as the wise adjudicator is reminiscent of Solomon, who chose between the two women who claimed an infant as their child.

3-SECOND BIOGRAPHIES
ZEUS/JUPITER
King of Olympus, god of the sky
See page 32

APOLLO
God of the sun, music and poetry
See page 42

APHRODITE/VENUS
Goddess of love and beauty
See page 50

DIONYSUS/BACCHUS
God of wine and theatre, son of Zeus
See page 56

30-SECOND TEXT
Emma Griffiths

Adonis' incandescent beauty has goddesses fighting over him.

OEDIPUS

the 30-second mythology

King Laius of Thebes learned

from an oracle that if his wife Jocasta bore a son, the son would kill him. So when Jocasta gave birth to a boy, he was left exposed in the wilderness to die or be lost forever. But the boy was found and was given to the childless King and Queen of Corinth. As an adult, Oedipus went to the Delphic Oracle to discover whether or not he was legitimate. The oracle predicted that he would kill his father and sleep with his mother. Rather than returning to Corinth, to whose king and queen he still assumed he had been born, Oedipus, horrified at the prophecy, fled. Near Thebes, he experienced the first recorded case of road rage with a traveller, who turned out to be King Laius of Thebes – Oedipus' real father. Oedipus, unaware of the person's identity, killed him and proceeded to Thebes, astride the entrance to which loomed the Sphinx, a monster with a lion's body, a woman's face and a bird's wings. The Sphinx had posed a riddle, and while it remained unsolved, she would devour Thebans entering or leaving the city. Oedipus answered the riddle, causing the Sphinx to self-destruct. He was rewarded with the now vacant throne and the hand of the late king's wife, Jocasta. Years later the truth of who he really was and what he had done emerged.

3-SECOND MUSE
Oedipus was fated to kill his father and marry his mother, and unwittingly did so.

3-MINUTE ODYSSEY
One version of the Sphinx's riddle was: What has one voice and walks on four feet and two feet and three feet? Oedipus answered: A human being. For a baby is four-footed, an adult is two-footed and an old person walking with a staff is three-footed. The Riddle of Man, as it is called, is known in many countries.

RELATED MYTH
Judas Iscariot is another well-known example of an unfortunate individual who was said to have killed his own father and married his mother.

3-SECOND BIOGRAPHIES
ODYSSEUS/ULYSSES
Greek hero renowned for his intelligence
See page 102

THESEUS
Greek hero who killed the Minotaur
See page 106

PERSEUS
Greek hero who killed the Gorgon Medusa
See page 108

OEDIPUS COMPLEX
Psychoanalytical term for every boy's childhood drive to kill his father in order to be able to have sex with his mother
See page 142

30-SECOND TEXT
William Hansen

Freud saw Oedipus' tragic story as a disguised expression of a universal male wish.

ANTIGONE

the 30-second mythology

Antigone was the daughter of the incestuous relationship between Oedipus and Jocasta. After her father's incest was exposed, a great war ensued, in which one of Antigone's brothers, Polyneices, led an army against Thebes, which was defended by her other brother, Eteocles. The brothers killed each other in combat, and Antigone vowed to give honourable burial to Polyneices, despite the Theban King Creon's commandment that the body should be left exposed to dogs and birds. Antigone, convinced of the morality of her actions, continued with the burial plan but was captured and brought before Creon. In her defence Antigone claimed that the law of the gods trumped the law of man; Creon insisted that the laws of the state must triumph. He thereby set up the major theme of the choice between duty to the state and personal morality. He ordered Antigone to be buried alive in a cave. Antigone hanged herself just before Creon's son Haemon, who had been engaged to marry her, came to the cave. In a suicidal rage Haemon lunged at his father, then killed himself. Queen Eurydice of Thebes, wife of Creon, learning of her son's death, also killed herself, leaving Creon all alone.

3-SECOND MUSE
Antigone attempted to honour her treacherous dead brother and was accordingly sentenced to death.

3-MINUTE ODYSSEY
Sophocles' play is the first one solely about Antigone, but Euripides wrote a lost play on the topic. From a summary we learn that Creon had ordered his son Haemon to execute the girl. Instead, Haemon hid her in the countryside, where she bore his child. Later, when attending the games in Thebes, Antigone's son was recognized. Realizing that people knew Antigone was still alive, Haemon, fearing his father's wrath, killed both her and himself.

RELATED MYTH
The story of 'Antigone' has been imitated by the French playwright Jean Anouilh (1943), the German dramatist Bertolt Brecht (1948), the Spanish writer María Zambrano (1967) and the Irish poet and writer Seamus Heaney (2007).

3-SECOND BIOGRAPHY
OEDIPUS
King of Thebes
Page 116

30-SECOND TEXT
Barry B. Powell

Oedipus' is the ultimate dysfunctional family in classical mythology. His daughter Antigone hangs herself after her brothers have killed each other.

ORPHEUS & EURYDICE

the 30-second mythology

Orpheus was the greatest of singer-songwriters. When he sang to the music of his lyre, not only people but also birds and beasts, trees, rivers and rocks gathered to hear him. His beloved, Eurydice, died of a snake bite on their wedding day. Orpheus descended to the underworld and played to Hades and Persephone, pleading to have her back. The gods of death, while ordinarily implacable, were for once moved. But they allowed Eurydice to leave Hades on one condition: that Orpheus must walk on ahead and not look back to check whether she was following. Tellers of the tale have never agreed on why Orpheus, having almost reached the light of day, turned to look back and thereby see Eurydice vanish for the second and final time. There is an alternative version, according to which Orpheus was given not Eurydice but an illusion. The heartbroken poet retired to the wilderness to sing of his grief. In the end he was killed by the Maenads, wild female followers of Dionysus, who tore him to pieces and threw his head, still singing, into the River Hebrus.

3-SECOND MUSE
The most tragic love story of Greek myth is that of the great musician Orpheus and his double loss of Eurydice.

3-MINUTE ODYSSEY
The Greeks believed that Orpheus had been a real ancient poet and religious teacher. Orphism, a religion of its own, arose around his name. It centred on reincarnation and purification of the soul by ascetic practices. Some modern scholars think the original Orpheus may have been a shaman, a tribal magician who claimed that he had the ability to travel back and forth to the land of the dead.

RELATED MYTH
The katabasis, or underworld descent, is a common mythic motif. In Finnish legend the mother of the hero Lemminkäinen succeeded in bringing her son back from the underworld.

3-SECOND BIOGRAPHIES
DIONYSUS/BACCHUS
God of wine and madness
See page 56

HADES
At once god of the underworld and the underworld itself
See page 82

30-SECOND TEXT
Geoffrey Miles

The failure of Orpheus and Eurydice to enjoy their love until united in death is the ultimate tragic love story.

JASON & MEDEA

the 30-second mythology

Jason was heir to the throne, but he was ordered by his uncle, Pelias, to capture the Golden Fleece, which was the gold fleece of a winged ram from Colchis, or modern Georgia. In the *Argonautica*, the main source of the myth, Apollonius of Rhodes tells how, with the help of a group of heroes called the Argonauts, Jason reached Colchis but was set impossible tasks by the king, Aeetes. The king's daughter, Medea, fell in love with Jason. When Jason promised to marry her, she used her magic to help him win the Golden Fleece. Later, on their return to Greece, she killed the giant Talos, who was keeping the ship from returning home. But after moving to Corinth, Jason left Medea for the king's daughter, and in the version made famous by Euripides, Medea took revenge by killing her two children by Jason. Jason's story fades at this point, with a prophecy that he would be killed by a plank from his old ship, the *Argo*. Medea left Corinth and was welcomed in Athens by King Aegeus. She fled Athens after trying to kill Aegeus' stepson, Theseus, and travelled east, where her son, Medus, founded the race of 'Medes'. After her death Medea was transported to the Elysian Fields and married Achilles.

3-SECOND MUSE
Medea's magical powers helped Jason capture the Golden Fleece. They married and had two children, but Jason later abandoned her, and in revenge Medea killed their offspring.

3-MINUTE ODYSSEY
Witchcraft was traditionally associated with foreign, distant places where the rules of civilization did not apply. Medea was the niece of the sorceress Circe, who beguiled Odysseus in Homer's *Odyssey*. In some versions Jason and Medea visited Circe to be purified after killing Medea's brother Absyrtus during their escape from Colchis. Medea's name means 'the schemer', and Jason's name means 'healer'. Medicine and magic were closely linked in the ancient world.

RELATED MYTH
Like Medea, Clytemnestra took revenge on her husband in part because he, Agamemnon, came home from Troy with a mistress, Cassandra, though also because he, like Medea, had sacrificed their daughter Iphigenia.

3-SECOND BIOGRAPHIES
APOLLO
Olympian god of the sun, music and poetry
See page 42

ACHILLES
Greatest hero of the Trojan War, son of the nymph Thetis
See page 98

THESEUS
Heroic founder of Athens, illegitimate son of King Aegeus
See page 106

30-SECOND TEXT
Emma Griffiths

Medea, a woman scorned, takes revenge on Jason by killing their two children.

AJAX

the 30-second mythology

Ajax was second only to Achilles as the greatest Greek fighter at Troy. He was the son of Telamon and is often referred to as the Telamonian Ajax or 'the greater Ajax', as opposed to fellow Greek fighter Ajax, son of Oileus, or 'the lesser Ajax'. Often depicted holding a gigantic shield made of seven cow-hides with a layer of bronze, Ajax was chosen by lot to meet Hector in a duel that lasted a day. The heralds eventually called a draw. When Achilles died, Ajax and Odysseus worked together to recover his body. In a rhetorical competition to determine who deserved Achilles' armour, which had been made by the god Hephaestus, Odysseus easily outshone Ajax and won the prize. Athena, Odysseus' patron god, then drove Ajax mad, causing him to kill a flock of sheep that he imagined to be the Greek leaders and judges. When he recovered and saw himself covered in sheep's blood, the humiliated Ajax went away along the loud-resounding sea and fell upon his sword. When Odysseus saw the soul of Ajax in Hades, Ajax would not speak to him and turned silently away.

Ajax's great physical might is in contrast to his occasional frailty of mind. He ultimately kills himself.

DIDO

the 30-second mythology

Dido (perhaps Phoenician for 'virgin'), was the legendary founder and first Queen of Carthage, in modern Tunisia. According to archaeology, Carthage was founded sometime around 825 BC, and Dido might have been an actual historical figure. When Dido's brother Pygmalion killed her husband, Sychaeus, Dido fled from Tyre on the eastern coast of the Mediterranean and sailed far away to the coast of North Africa. There she founded Carthage. According to Virgil's *Aeneid*, the Trojan hero Aeneas landed in Africa after fleeing the burning Troy. His mother Venus (Aphrodite) caused Dido to fall in love with the stranger, and they had a passionate relationship. Eventually, Jupiter (Zeus) sent Mercury (Hermes) to command Aeneas to proceed with his mission of founding the Roman race. As Aeneas sailed away, Dido mounted a pyre and killed herself upon it. In her dying words she cursed the Trojan and all his descendants, the Romans. From his departing ship Aeneas saw the distant glow of Dido's burning pyre. In the second and third centuries BC, the Punic Wars, between the Romans and the Carthaginians, were the bloodiest conflicts of the ancient world.

3-SECOND MUSE
When Aeneas abandoned Dido, the beautiful Queen of Carthage, in order to fulfil his destiny of founding the Roman race, she killed herself and cursed his descendants.

3-MINUTE ODYSSEY
Aeneas saw Dido when he visited his father in the underworld. He reached out to her and apologized, but Dido turned away to join the spirit of her husband, Sychaeus. The romantic tale of Dido and Aeneas became highly popular after the Renaissance. Christopher Marlowe's first play, *Dido, Queen of Carthage*, treated the theme (1594), and it inspired many operas, including works by Francesco Cavalli (1641), Henry Purcell (1689), Niccolò Piccinni (1770) and Hector Berlioz (1860).

RELATED MYTH
Tragic love affairs are common in Greek myth, especially the stories of Jason and Medea and of Helen and Paris, on which the story of Aeneas and Dido is partly based. Odysseus, too, was detained by two demi-gods who fell in love with him: the witch Circe, with whom he spent a year, and the nymph Calypso, who kept him for seven years on her island.

3-SECOND BIOGRAPHIES
TROY
City on the Hellespont, site of the Trojan War
See page 88

AENEAS
Trojan prince, ancestor of the Romans
See page 104

VIRGIL
Roman poet, author of the *Aeneid*
See page 128

30-SECOND TEXT
Barry B. Powell

Dido is unlucky in love. Her brother murders her husband, and her lover, Aeneas, leaves her.

15 October, 70 BC
Born in Andes, near Mantua

42 BC
Began to write *Eclogues*

39–38 BC
Eclogues published

37–29 BC
Composed the *Georgics*

29–19 BC
Composed the *Aeneid*

19 BC
Aeneid finished by Lucius Varius Rufus and Plotius Tocca (Virgil's literary executors) at the command of Emperor Augustus and later published posthumously, despite the poet's wish that it be burned.

21 September, 19 BC
Died at Brundisium (modern Brindisi)

1697
Aeneid translated by John Dryden

1883
Eclogues translated and illustrated by the artist Samuel Palmer

2006
Aeneid translated by Robert Fagles

VIRGIL

Virgil (Publius Vergilius Maro)

was one of ancient Rome's greatest poets, master of both pastoral and epic, and a great influence on modern Western literature. Dante made him his guide and mentor through hell and most of purgatory. Virgil coined some iconic phrases, of which the best known is *omnia vincit amor* (love conquers all).

After spurning a career in law, Virgil, like Ovid, turned to poetry, at which he was very successful despite suffering from chronic bad health and shabby treatment from a succession of gilded youths. He is best known for the pastorals the *Eclogues* and the *Georgics* and the epic the *Aeneid*. The *Eclogues* and the *Georgics* are both ostensibly concerned with aspects of life on the land but are laden with symbolic allusions to current politics in Rome. It was Virgil who constructed the idea of Arcadia, the idyllic, golden pastoral paradise idealized in the European Romantic movement, yet which also contains Death. Virgil's position as a gatekeeper between old and new is supported by Book 4 of the *Eclogues*, which Christians interpreted as prefiguring the birth of Christ, and Book 6, which covers the myth of Orpheus, pagan god of death and rebirth.

Virgil's greatest and most influential work is undoubtedly the *Aeneid*. Commissioned by Emperor Augustus, it not only was the literary link between ancient Greek and Roman traditions but also became the expression of Rome's identity – part history, part myth. Drawing inspiration from Homer's *Iliad* and *Odyssey*, it is the story of Aeneas, the son of Anchises, Prince of Troy, and the goddess Aphrodite. When the Trojans lost the war, Aeneas took flight with his father and a band of supporters, inspired by a prophecy that claimed he would found a powerful new race. After stopping off at Carthage – where he wooed and then spurned Dido, initiating the Punic Wars – and Sicily, he finally settled in Latium. After his death, Aeneas was deified. His descendants Romulus and Remus eventually established Rome. The Emperors Julius and Augustus traced their ancestry back to Aeneas, thereby linking them with the Olympian gods and thus conferring on Rome a divine pedigree.

PHAETHON

the 30-second mythology

3-SECOND MUSE
Phaethon, son of the sun god, died trying to emulate his father by driving his father's chariot with the sun across the sky.

3-MINUTE ODYSSEY
The warning 'be careful what you wish for' is also to be found in the story of Semele, one of Zeus' lovers. Zeus' vengeful wife, Hera, tricked Semele into asking Zeus to show her how he had first appeared to Hera. Zeus had agreed to do whatever Semele, unlike Hera, asked, and although he tried to talk her out of it, he had no choice but to acquiesce. As a mortal, Semele was incinerated when Zeus revealed himself as pure light.

Together with Icarus, Phaethon ('the shining one') was the original tearaway who met a tragic end. According to one version, his mother, Klymene, told him he was the child of Helios, the sun god, but Phaethon did not believe her, so Helios promised to give him anything to prove he was his father. According to another version, Phaethon's friends doubted that he was the son of a god, so he set out to get proof. When Phaethon's father offered to grant him any wish, Phaethon asked for the reins to the chariot that Helios drove every day across the sky, a chariot pulled by winged horses. Although he tried to dissuade Phaethon from this suicidal request, Helios could not rescind the offer and could only offer vain advice to his son. The horses proved uncontrollable. As Phaethon careered through the sky, the chariot came too close to the earth and burned the lands of Africa. Zeus, afraid that the entire earth would be destroyed, struck Phaethon with a thunderbolt, and his body fell into the River Eridanos. Like Icarus, who flew too close to the sun, Phaethon serves as a warning against the recklessness of youth. Helios' granddaughter, Medea, later drove the chariot more successfully when she used it to escape from Corinth after having killed her children.

RELATED MYTH
Being unable to rescind a blessing or vow echoes the biblical story of Isaac, who was tricked into giving the blessing intended for his firstborn, Esau, to his younger son, Jacob.

3-SECOND BIOGRAPHIES
ZEUS/JUPITER
King of Olympus, god of the sky
See page 32

ICARUS
Son of Daedalus, who flew too close to the sun
See page 132

30-SECOND TEXT
Emma Griffiths

Phaethon's youthful exuberance proves his undoing. The story tallies with the Greek ideal of moderation.

ICARUS

the 30-second mythology

Minos, the King of Crete, had imprisoned the brilliant inventor Daedalus, who was kept within the labyrinth that he himself had built at the king's request. Considering his options, Daedalus ruled out escape by land or sea, since Crete was an island and Minos controlled the seas. However, there was always a third option: the air. So Daedalus collected feathers and arranged them in winglike configurations, binding them together with twine and wax. He made one set for himself and another for his son, Icarus. When it was time to escape, Daedalus warned his son not to fly too low, where the humidity might weigh down his wings, or too high, where the sun might melt their wax. Then the two arose in flight, son following father. Seeing them, a few people were amazed and assumed they were gods. Icarus, however, became so exhilarated by the experience that he soared ever higher, until the sun melted the wax of his wings, and he plummeted to his death into the waters below. The sea in which he drowned became known as the Icarian Sea, and the nearby island where the grieving father buried his son was renamed Icaria.

3-SECOND MUSE
Icarus was a Greek youth whose artificial wings, held together by wax, disintegrated when he flew too close to the sun.

3-MINUTE ODYSSEY
The Icarian Sea probably got its name from the nearby island of Icaria, but how Icaria acquired its name is anybody's guess. According to the Icarus legend, the sea and the island were so called because Icarus drowned in the one and was interred on the other. Such aetiological motifs, which sometimes appear at the conclusion of traditional narratives, typically trace a feature of the world to a single event in the past.

RELATED MYTH
Humans in mythology who achieve the dream of flight less often employ their own synthetic wings than hitch a ride on a large bird. The earliest example is Etana (from Mesopotamia).

3-SECOND BIOGRAPHY
PHAETHON
Tragic youth who drove the sun's chariot
See page 130

30-SECOND TEXT
William Hansen

Icarus discovers, to his cost, that pride leads to a fall.

ACTAEON

the 30-second mythology

Actaeon was part of a famous dynasty. His mother, Autonoë, was the daughter of the Theban hero Cadmus, and his father was Aristaeus, a son of the god Apollo. Actaeon was educated by the centaur Chiron and became a famous hunter, sometimes said to be a companion of the goddess Artemis. In the main version of the myth, as told by Callimachus and Ovid, Actaeon offended the goddess by inadvertently coming upon her naked in the woods. Other versions claim that he boasted that he could hunt better than Artemis or that he was a suitor for the princess Semele, whom Zeus loved. Whatever the offence, the punishment was the same: Artemis turned him into a stag and drove his hounds mad so they tore him to pieces on Mount Cithaeron. On the same mountain Pentheus was torn to pieces for having insulted the god Dionysus, and the baby Oedipus was abandoned just after birth. In some tellings of the myth the hounds were so grief-stricken when they realized what they had done that Chiron made a statue of Actaeon to console them.

3-SECOND MUSE
A Greek mythological hunter who, having offended Artemis, was transformed into a stag and torn apart by his own hounds.

3-MINUTE ODYSSEY
Metamorphosis from human to animal is a common motif in myth. Callisto was turned into a bear after she had broken a vow to Artemis, and was then hunted until she died. Although many transformations were punishments, they could also be an act of salvation as when Procne and Philomela were turned into birds as they fled from Tereus, or when Zeus turned Io into a cow to hide her from the jealous rage of Hera.

RELATED MYTH
In the Ugaritic myth of Daniel and Aqhat, the goddess Anat killed the hunter Aqhat when he offended her by refusing a trade.

3-SECOND BIOGRAPHIES
ZEUS/JUPITER
King of Olympus, god of the sky
See page 32

ARTEMIS/DIANA
Daughter of Zeus and Leto, virgin goddess of the hunt
See page 46

DIONYSUS/BACCHUS
God of wine and theatre, son of Zeus,
See page 56

30-SECOND TEXT
Emma Griffiths

As punishment for having dared see her naked, Actaeon the hunter is turned by Artemis into the hunted.

LEGACY

complex In psychology, a termed coined by C. G. Jung to describe a set of emotionally charged experiences caused by either a childhood experience (Freud) or an innate archetype (Jung). The complex can express itself in many ways, usually symbolically. Mental health requires the recognition of the complex. Eventually, the term was used by Freudians exclusively, as in Oedipus complex.

hypersexuality Sexual activity in either men or women that affects normal social functioning or causes distress. The term replaces the traditional, mythologically rooted terms 'nymphomania' and 'satyriasis'.

neurotic A person suffering from a neurosis, which in psychoanalytic terms means an unconscious emotional conflict, going back to childhood, that manifests itself in adulthood in ways that overtly have nothing to do with childhood but that are in fact disguised expressions of unresolved sexual and emotional tensions. Traditionally, neuroses are treated through analysis.

nymphomania Term that used to be applied to what was considered excessive sexuality in women. It then came to be seen as a symptom of a larger personality disorder. It is now called hypersexuality or just sex addiction.

Oedipal stage In Freud's stages of pyschosexual development, the Oedipal (or phallic) stage occurs between the ages of three and five, and describes the stage at which children become possessive of the parent of the opposite sex, while seeing the parent of the same sex as a rival. Freud considered the Oedipal stage – a term he used for girls as well as for boys – as the key one for the development of personality and as the key, though by no means the only, source of adult psychological problems.

personality disorder Any one of a range of disorders which keep an individual from dealing flexibly and sensibly with the varying situations that life presents. Those suffering from a personality disorder react rigidly and unbendingly to situations. The major disorders include paranoia, schizophrenia, histrionics and anti-social behaviour. A person may suffer from more than one disorder.

pre-Oedipal stage Freud's unbending view was that the key stage of psychosexual development was the Oedipal stage. His once-close disciple and even heir, Otto Rank, came to maintain that the key stage is in fact pre-Oedipal, or the stage right after birth. For Freud, the fundamental relationship in the Oedipal stage is that between a child and the parent of the same sex. For Rank, the fundamental relationship in the pre-Oedipal stage is that between a child, boy or girl, and the mother. Where for Freud the child seeks to replace the parent of the same sex, for Rank the child seeks to remain united with the mother in the womb. The trauma that determines one's personality comes not at age three but at birth. Freudians today, while still considering Rank a heretic, have long since come to give at least as much importance to the pre-Oedipal stage as to the Oedipal one.

satyriasis Term once used for the male counterpart to nymphomania. As in nymphomania, excessive sexuality was seen as a symptom of a broader psychological malady. This term, too, has now been replaced by hypersexuality or sex addiction.

NARCISSISM

the 30-second mythology

Narcissus was an exceptionally attractive youth who, rejecting both males and females, was punished by one spurned male by being made to fall in love with his own reflection in the water. Narcissus had no understanding of reflection and so did not realize that he was beholding only a mirror of himself and not his actual self. Unable to grasp hold of his reflection yet unable to break the attraction, he withered away and died. He was turned into a flower, the narcissus. The term 'narcissism' refers to excessive self-absorption and obliviousness to others. The term was coined by the English physician and pioneering sexologist Havelock Ellis to refer to excessive masturbation, but was expanded and enriched into a psychological state by the far more theoretical Sigmund Freud. 'Healthy narcissism' is the common current term for sufficient attention to oneself and not just to others. Narcissism as a personality disorder refers to preoccupation with oneself at the expense of others. For Freud, narcissism as an illness is the carrying of healthy narcissism to an extreme.

30-SECOND TEXT
Robert A. Segal

3-SECOND MUSE
Narcissism is the name for the state of persons excessively absorbed with themselves. It is more extreme than sheer vanity, pride or self-confidence.

3-MINUTE ODYSSEY
The source of narcissism remains moot. One common psychoanalytic explanation is the denial of love during early years. Unloved as a child, the adult narcissist in turn can feel no love for others. Narcissists are incapable of empathy. They are often charming on the surface but in fact are manipulative, cunning and deceitful. The concept of narcissism has been applied to whole cultures, most famously to contemporary America by Christopher Lasch in *The Culture of Narcissism* (1979).

While Narcissus' self-love is the result of a curse, Freud offers a scientific explanation of the phenomenon generally.

OEDIPUS COMPLEX

the 30-second mythology

3-SECOND MUSE
'Oedipus complex' is
Freud's name for the drive
in all boys from three to
five to kill their fathers in
order to have sex with
their mothers.

3-MINUTE ODYSSEY
Freud stalwartly made the
Oedipus complex the heart
of his psychology. But
since his day, the focus
of even mainstream
psychoanalysis has shifted
from the Oedipal stage,
which for Freud centred
on the conflict between
sons and fathers, to the
pre-Oedipal stage, which
focuses on the relations,
by no means hostile,
between children and
mothers. At the same
time the term 'Oedipus
complex' has come to be
applied to females as well
as to males. The term
'Electra complex' is no
longer used.

The subject of, above all,
Sophocles' play *Oedipus Rex* (*Oedipus the
King*), Oedipus is perhaps the most famous
human figure from Greek mythology, though
his fame stems partly from the appropriation
of his saga by Freud. As a victim of a curse on
his house, King Laius of Thebes was warned
that if he fathered a son, the son would one
day kill him. Laius accepted the prophecy and
instructed a servant to kill the infant, whose
conception had stemmed from an episode of
drunkenness and so loss of self-control. Laius
thought that, by having his son killed, he could
outwit the prophecy. Alas, Oedipus was saved,
was raised elsewhere, and as an adult fulfilled
the prophecy, which now included incest with
his mother. Even though Oedipus was seemingly
the victim of Fate, which he, like his father,
tried vainly to circumvent, Freud made him
the victimizer. For Freud, as presented in *The
Interpretation of Dreams* (1900), Oedipus, as
an adult, fulfilled the childhood drive in all
males: to kill their fathers in order to secure
sexual access to their mothers. The 'Oedipus
complex' is normal in childhood but neurotic
when carried on into adulthood, even if never
outwardly fulfilled.

3-SECOND BIOGRAPHIES
OEDIPUS
King of Thebes; he killed his
father and married his mother
See page 116

SOPHOCLES
Greek playwright, author of
Oedipus Rex
See page 146

30-SECOND TEXT
Robert A. Segal

*All boys naturally
want to kill their
fathers and sleep
with their mothers ...
so says Freud.*

ELECTRA COMPLEX

the 30-second mythology

3-SECOND MUSE
'Electra complex' names
the stage of development
in which all girls fantasize
about killing their mother
in order to get sexual
access to their father.

3-MINUTE ODYSSEY
The term 'Electra complex'
fits the phenomenon it
names less well than the
term 'Oedipus complex'
fits its phenomenon.
Whereas the mythological
character Oedipus actually
killed his father and then
proceeded to marry his
mother, Electra was not
the one who killed her
mother, and her father
was already dead. Oedipus
did the very things that,
consciously, he least
wanted to do, whereas
Electra did consciously
want her mother dead.

In Greek mythology, Electra was the daughter of King Agamemnon and Queen Clytemnestra. Of her siblings, the most important were her elder sister, Iphigenia, and her brother Orestes. Agamemnon was the leader of the Greek army that fought at Troy. While Agamemnon was away, Clytemnestra took a lover, Aegisthus. Together, they killed Agamemnon upon his triumphant return home. Clytemnestra hated him because he had sacrificed Iphigenia so that the Greek forces could get the wind needed to sail to Troy. She also hated him because he had come home with a mistress, Cassandra. Electra sided with her father despite his actions, and she persuaded Orestes to kill their mother. It was not Freud but his rival, Carl Gustav Jung, who coined the term 'complex' and later, in 1913, the specific instance 'Electra complex', by which he meant the universal drive in girls from three to five to seek sex with their fathers and to kill their mothers, who stand in the way. Freud took the term complex from Jung and coined the term 'Oedipus complex', to which the Electra complex was meant to be the female counterpart. Once Freud and Jung split, Freud abandoned the term Electra complex and preferred to use 'Oedipus complex' for both sexes.

3-SECOND BIOGRAPHY
OEDIPUS
King of Thebes; he killed his
father and married his mother
See page 116

30-SECOND TEXT
Robert A. Segal

All girls naturally want to kill their mothers and sleep with their fathers ... so says Freud and so originally said Jung as well.

nus near
son of a
chant

ze at the
sia festival,
schylus

ged

one

409 BC
Wrote *Philoctetes*
and *Electra*

406 BC
Wrote *Oedipus Coloneus*
(*Oedipus at Colonus*)

405 BC
Died

401 BC
Oedipus Coloneus
first staged

1954
Oedipus the King
translated by David
Grene; *Oedipus at
Colonus* translated by
Robert Fitzgerald;
Antigone translated by
Elizabeth Wyckoff

1954
The Three Theban Plays:
*Antigone, Oedipus the
King, Oedipus at Colonus*
translated by Robert
Fagles

SOPHOCLES

Following Aeschylus, Sophocles
enjoyed a successful fifty-year career as a
dramatist in Athens. Over 120 plays are ascribed
to him, although only seven, together with a
few fragments, are extant. He won around
twenty-four prizes at the city's annual drama
festival, the Dionysia, claiming first prize from
under the nose of Aeschylus with his first entry
at the age of twenty-eight. Aristotle cites
Oedipus Rex (*Oedipus the King*) as the exemplar
of the perfectly structured tragic play.

Like Aeschylus, Sophocles was an innovator.
He added a third actor to Aeschylus' two,
thereby increasing the dialogue and decreasing
the importance of the chorus. He replaced the
linked trilogy with three separate plays, even
if still on the same subject. His three plays on
Oedipus – *Oedipus the King* (*Oedipus Rex*),
Oedipus at Colonus (*Oedipus Coloneus*) and
Antigone – are not, strictly, a linked trilogy.

Many of Sophocles' themes are the same as
those of Aeschylus. Humans must recognize
Fate and the power of the gods. Humans
delude themselves in imagining that they can
determine their destiny. Yet they must still
accept responsibility for their actions. In the
most famous of Sophocles' tragedies and in
fact of all Greek tragedies, *Oedipus the King*,
Oedipus is wrong to think that he can avert
his fate, which is to kill his father and to
marry his mother. His fate is the consequence
of a curse on the house of his forebears.

Yet Oedipus' fall stems not only from his
fated actions, for which he cannot be held
responsible, but from his freely chosen
actions – once he has become King of Thebes
in place of his killed father, Oedipus deems
himself god-like. He assumes that on his
own he can end the plague that has befallen
Thebes. His fall comes not with the plague
but with his insistence on discovering the
culprit, who turns out to be Oedipus himself.
He falls not because he long ago acted out his
'Oedipus complex' but because, decades later,
he spurns the gods, as spoken for by the
prophet Teiresias. For the consequences of his
arrogance he is altogether held responsible.

Yet for Sophocles, as for Aeschylus, from
suffering can come wisdom, and Oedipus
is the most conspicuous example in ancient
tragedy of someone who through suffering
is transformed from a most clever fellow to
a most wise one.

From his mid fifties on, Sophocles took
more interest in civil matters, becoming an
ordained priest and an administrator in city
government. Sophocles failed to shine in
any of these roles, and it is as a playwright
that he is best remembered.

NYMPHOMANIA

the 30-second mythology

Nymphs were nubile female

figures who lived away from civilization and its strictures. They were to be found above all in trees, mountains, rivers and springs. They were more than human but were, at most, lower-ranking goddesses. They were not immortal and sometimes died when the natural phenomenon they inhabited died. They lived in groups and only occasionally were identified individually. Nymphs were beautiful and care-free and enjoyed physical pleasures, including sex, but by no means were always promiscuous. Some were celibate. Others shunned sex with males. Still others sought sex with males and, as with the youth Hylas, could lure them to their deaths. The term 'nymphomania' is used derisively for females whose sexual desire is supposedly insatiable. Strictly, the term is medical and refers to a condition that is rare and is symptomatic of some mental disorder. For males, there is the far less well-known medical term 'satyriasis', which likewise takes its name from Greek mythology. Satyrs were half men, half goats known for their licentiousness. Satyrs and nymphs sometimes had sex with each other.

3-SECOND MUSE
'Nymphomania' is a derogatory term for the supposedly excessive sexuality of some females, but more precisely names a psychological malady of which sexual insatiability is only a symptom.

3-MINUTE ODYSSEY
The more common term today for nymphomania is 'hypersexuality', which applies to males as well as to females. At what point sexuality becomes hyper is debatable and varies conspicuously with time and place. Some experts deem hypersexuality an addiction and want it added to the official list of psychiatric ailments. Hypersexuality has been attributed by some to childhood sexual abuse, by others to obsessive-compulsive disorder. The compulsiveness for sex is a mere symptom of hypersexuality.

30-SECOND TEXT
Robert A. Segal

The nymphs of classical mythology were not so insatiable as their modern-day counterparts.

PYGMALION EFFECT

the 30-second mythology

3-SECOND MUSE
The term 'Pygmalion effect', while named after a sculptor whose sculpture comes to life, refers to the change that others' expectations can have on their subjects.

3-MINUTE ODYSSEY
In the *Metamorphoses* Ovid describes the transformations of humans and also nymphs into animals and plants. The transformation of Pygmalion's sculpture into a living female, through the power of love, is typically Ovidian. The rather less romantic Robert Merton (1910–2003) coined the term 'self-fulfilling prophecy', by which the 'Pygmalion effect' is now far better known. His example is of a solvent bank that goes bankrupt as a result of false rumours of its insolvency, rumours that lead customers to withdraw their money.

In the *Metamorphoses* Ovid tells the story of a sculptor named Pygmalion, who, revolted by the pervasiveness of prostitutes, forswore sex and lived as a celibate. But he sculpted an ivory statue of a beautiful virgin and fell in love with the statue. When he returned home from a festival to Venus, he kissed the statue, which, thanks to Venus, immediately came to life. The link to the term 'Pygmalion effect', coined by the American sociologist Robert Merton, is tricky. Well before George Bernard Shaw's most famous play, *Pygmalion*, appeared in 1912, there had been English comedies in which a married sculptor created a beautiful female who then came alive. Not his but her name became Pygmalion. Writing not a comedy but a comic satire on the rigidity of class, Shaw made Pygmalion, renamed Eliza Doolittle, a living person from the start. The transformation in his play is not from statue to living being but from cockney flower girl to aristocrat. The transformation succeeds less because of what she does and more because of her acceptance as an aristocrat by high society. The 'effect' means the effect that others' expectations, negative as well as positive, can have on their subjects.

3-SECOND BIOGRAPHY
OVID
Greek playwright, author of *Metamorphoses*
See page 70

30-SECOND TEXT
Robert A. Segal

The notion of 'living up to other people's expectations' is very different from the original myth of Pygmalion.

APPENDICES

RESOURCES

BOOKS

Ancient Goddesses: The Myths and the Evidence
Lucy Goodison and Christine Morris
(University of Wisconsin Press, 1999)

Anthology of Classical Myth: Primary Sources in Translation
Stephen M. Trzaskoma et al.
(Hackett, 2004)

Aphrodite
Monica S. Cyrino
(Routledge, 2010)

Apollo
Fritz Graf
(Routledge, 2009)

Apollodorus' Library and Hyginus' Fabulae: Two Handbooks of Greek Mythology
R. Scott Smith and Stephen M. Trzaskoma
(Hackett, 2007)

Art and Myth in Ancient Greece
Thomas H. Carpenter
(Thames & Hudson, 1991)

Athena
Susan Deacy
(Routledge, 2008)

The Cambridge Companion to Greek Mythology
Roger D. Woodard (ed.)
(Cambridge University Press, 2007)

Classical Myth (seventh edn)
Barry B. Powell
(Prentice Hall, 2011)

Classical Mythology: A Guide to the Mythical World of the Greeks and Romans
William Hansen
(Oxford University Press, 2005)

Classical Mythology: A Very Short Introduction
Helen Morales
(Oxford University Press, 2007)

Classical Mythology in English Literature: A Critical Anthology
Geoffrey Miles (ed.)
(Routledge, 1999)

The Complete World of Greek Mythology
Richard Buxton
(Thames & Hudson, 2004)

The Dictionary of Classical Mythology
Pierre Grimal, trans. A. R. Maxwell-Hyslop
(Blackwell, 1986)

Dionysus
Richard Seaford
(Routledge, 2006)

Greek Mythology, An Introduction
Fritz Graf, trans. Thomas Marier
(Johns Hopkins University Press, 1993)

A Handbook of Greek Mythology
Herbert J. Rose
(Methuen, first edn 1928; sixth edn, 1958)

Heracles
Emma Stafford
(Routledge, 2011)

Medea
Emma Griffiths
(Routledge, 2006)

The Meridian Handbook of Classical Mythology (originally *Crowell's Handbook of Classical Mythology* [Crowell, 1970])
Edward Tripp
(Meridian, 1974)

The Mirror of the Gods: How Renaissance Artists Rediscovered the Pagan Gods
Malcolm Bull
(Oxford University Press, 2005)

The Modern Construction of Myth
Andrew Von Hendy
(Indiana University Press, 2002)

Myth: Critical Concepts in Literary and Cultural Studies (4 vols)
Robert A. Segal (ed.)
(Routledge, 2007)

Myth: A Very Short Introduction
Robert A. Segal
(Oxford University Press, 2004)

Myths of the Greeks and Romans (rev. edn)
Michael Grant
(Penguin, 1995)

The Myths of Rome
Timothy P. Wiseman
(University of Exeter Press, 2004)

The Nature of Greek Myths
Geoffrey S. Kirk
(Penguin, 1974)

Oedipus
Lowell Edmunds
(Routledge, 2006)

Perseus
Daniel Ogden
(Routledge, 2008)

Prometheus
Carol Dougherty
(Routledge, 2006)

RESOURCES

The Rise of Modern Mythology 1680–1860
Burton Feldman and Robert D. Richardson
(Indiana University Press, 1972)

Roman Myths
Michael Grant
(Penguin, 1973)

*The Routledge Handbook of Greek
Mythology* (based on H. J. Rose's
A Handbook of Greek Mythology)
Robin Hard
(Routledge, 2004)

A Short Introduction to Classical Myth
Barry B. Powell
(Prentice Hall, 2002)

*The Survival of the Pagan Gods: The
Mythological Tradition and its Place
in Renaissance Humanism and Art*
Jean Seznec
(Princeton University Press, 1953)

The Uses of Greek Mythology
Ken Dowden
(Routledge, 1992)

Zeus
Ken Dowden
(Routledge, 2006)

WEBSITES & LIBRARY COLLECTIONS

The Bryn Mawr Classical Review at http://ccat.
sas-upenn.edu/bmcr/arch.html
Richard Hamilton and James J. O'Donnell (eds).
A searchable archive of recent publications
pertaining to the classical world. The leading
review journal of classical studies.

Lexicon Iconographicum Mythologiae Classicae
(*LIMC*) (Zurich, 1981–99). Massive multi-volume
compilation of every representation of every
myth, with scholarly commentary in several
languages but mostly English. The single
leading resource for the study of myth and
art in the ancient world, invaluable but available
only in research libraries.

The Ovid Collection at the University of Virginia.
http://etext.lib.virginia.edu/latin/ovid/

The Perseus Project, ed. Gregory R. Crane et al.,
has thousands of links to texts, works of art,
maps, lexica and other aids to understanding
myth and the classical world.
http://www.perseus.tufts.edu

*Theoi Greek Mythology: Exploring Mythology in
Classical Literature and Art.*
http://www.theoi.com/

NOTES ON CONTRIBUTORS

Viv Croot is a writer with a particular interest in popularizing specialist subjects. Her fascination with the literature of classical Greece focuses on the *Iliad* and the *Odyssey* and their influence on the Western literary tradition. She is co-author of *Troy: Homer's Iliad Retold* (Barnes & Noble, 2004).

Susan Deacy is Senior Lecturer in Greek History and Literature at Roehampton University, London. Her work on Athena has led to an exploration of the range of figures with whom this especially adaptable of ancient religious personages is connected. Deacy is editor of the 'Gods and Heroes of the Ancient World' series for Routledge, and author of publications, including *A Traitor to her Sex? Athena the Trickster* (forthcoming, Oxford University Press).

Emma Griffiths is a Lecturer in Greek at the University of Manchester. She has published on many aspects of Greek mythology and drama, and is currently working on a book about children in Greek tragedy.

William Hansen is Professor Emeritus of Classical Studies and Folklore and formerly co-director of the Mythology Studies programme at Indiana University, Bloomington. His books include *Anthology of Ancient Greek Popular Literature* (Indiana University Press, 1998), *Ariadne's Thread: A Guide to International Tales Found in Classical Literature* (Cornell University Press, 2002) and *Classical Mythology: A Guide to the Mythical World of the Greeks and Romans* (Oxford University Press, 2005).

Geoffrey Miles is Senior Lecturer in English at Victoria University of Wellington, New Zealand, with a special interest in the transformations of the classical world and classical myth in English literature. He is the editor of *Classical Mythology in English Literature* (Routledge, 1999), and co-author of *The Snake-Haired Muse* (Victoria University Press, 2011), a study of the use of myth by the New Zealand poet James K. Baxter.

Barry B. Powell is Halls-Bascom Professor of Classics Emeritus at University of Wisconsin–Madison. His books include *Classical Myth* (Prentice Hall, 2011), *Writing: Theory and History of the Technology of Civilization* (Wiley/Blackwell, 2009), and *Homer and the Origin of the Greek Alphabet* (Cambridge University Press, 1991). He is co-author (with Ian Morris) of *A New Companion to Homer* (Brill, 1997), and *The Greeks: History, Culture, and Society* (Prentice Hall, 2009).

Robert A. Segal is Sixth Century Chair in Religious Studies at the University of Aberdeen, Scotland. He is a leading authority on approaches to myth and is the author of *Myth: A Very Short Introduction* (Oxford University Press, 2004) and *Theorizing about Myth* (University of Massachusetts Press, 1999). He also edits the 'Theorists of Myth' series for Routledge.

INDEX

A

Acheron, the River 13, 61, 82
Achilles 38, 88, 94, 95, 98–9, 104, 122, 124
Actaeon 46, 112, 134–5
adamantine sickle 12, 18, 22
Adonis 48, 50, 114–15
Aegeus, King 106, 122
aegis 30, 38
Aeneas 50, 54, 66, 72, 94, 102, 104–5, 126, 129
Aeneid 94, 104, 126, 128, 129
Aeschylus 74, 85, 98, 147
Agamemnon, King of Greece 46, 88, 101, 122, 124, 144
Ageus, King of Athens 62
Ajax, the greater 52, 88, 94, 124–5
Ajax, the lesser 52, 124
Anchises 50, 94, 129
Andromeda 108
Antigone 118–19, 147
Aphrodite 12, 16, 22, 38, 40, 50–1, 62, 104, 114, 126, 129
Apollo 12, 24, 36, 42–3, 46, 54, 80, 90, 134
apples of the Hesperides 95
Ares 12, 16, 38, 40, 50, 114
Argonauts 60, 112, 122
Ariadne 62, 106
Arion 36, 48
Aristaeus 42, 134
Artemis 12, 42, 46–7, 112, 134
Athena 12, 18, 30, 34, 36, 38, 40, 50, 52–3, 56, 64, 74, 78, 79, 102, 108, 124
Augustus 71, 94, 128, 129

B

belt of Hippolyte 95

C

Callisto 134
Calypso 102, 114, 126
Cassandra 42, 52, 90, 122, 144
cattle of Geryon 95
Centaur 94
Cerberus 66–7, 82, 95, 96
Ceres (see *Demeter*)
Ceto 64, 94
Chaos 12, 13, 14–15, 18, 78
Charon 13, 31, 61, 79, 82
Chimaera 60, 66
Chiron 94, 134
Chrysoar 64
Circe 54, 102, 122, 126
Clytemnestra 122, 144
Colchis 60, 112
Corinth 78, 90
Crete 13, 32
Cronus 12, 13, 18, 22, 24, 30, 32, 34, 36, 48, 50, 74, 94
Cupid (see *Eros*)
Curetes 30, 32
Cyclopes 13, 30, 32, 42, 60, 68–9, 102

D

Daedelus 60, 62, 132
Dante 72, 129
Delos 42, 46
Delphi 24, 42, 79, 90–1, 95
Demeter 12, 30, 36, 48–9, 95, 101
Diana (see *Artemis*)
Dido 54, 104, 126–7, 129
Dione 30, 32, 50
Dionysus 12, 56–7, 94, 101, 112, 113, 120, 134

Dodona 30, 32, 79
Dyaus Pita 32

E

Echidna 60, 66, 113
Eclogues 128, 129
Electra complex 142, 144–5
Eleusinian Mysteries 30, 48
Eleusis 30, 48
Elysian Fields (see *Elysium*)
Elysium 13, 61, 94, 122
Erebus (see *Hades*)
Erichthonios 38, 52
Erinyes 12, 22, 74–5
Eros 13, 14, 16–17, 50
Erymanthian boar 95
Eteocles 113, 118
Euripides 84–5, 88, 101, 118, 122
Eurydice 66, 120–1
Eurydice of Thebes 118
Eurystheus 66, 95, 96

F

Freud, Sigmund 40, 140, 142
Furies (see *Erinyes*)

G

Gaia 12, 13, 14, 18–19, 22, 24, 30, 52, 60, 68, 74, 78, 86, 90
Georgics 128, 129
Giants 12, 22
Golden Fleece, the 60, 112, 122
Gorgons 64, 94, 108
Graeae 94, 108

H

Hades 13, 36, 48, 54, 61, 80, 82–3, 94, 95, 106, 108, 120, 124

Harpies 72–3
Hebe 34, 96
Hecate 31, 79
Hector 40, 88, 98
Helen 88, 126
Helios 40, 42, 130
Hephaestus 12, 26, 30, 34, 38–9, 40, 50, 52, 80, 124
Hera 12, 30, 32, 34–5, 38, 50, 95, 96, 113, 130, 134
Heracles 12, 34, 36, 52, 60, 66, 78, 94, 95, 96–7, 112
Hermes 12, 31, 50, 54–5, 56, 79, 82, 108, 112, 114, 126
Hesiod 12, 13, 14, 20–1, 22, 30, 44, 45, 60, 72, 78, 86
hind of Ceryneia 95
Homer 21, 24, 32, 44–5, 46, 78, 88, 94, 98, 129
horses of Diomedes 95
Hydra 66

I

Iapetus 24, 26
Icarus 130, 132–3
Iliad, the 44, 45, 88, 94, 95, 98, 104, 129
Iphigenia 46, 122, 144
Ithaca 36, 102

J

Jason 52, 60, 72, 85, 95, 112, 122–3, 126
Jocasta 116, 118
Juno (see *Hera*)
Jupiter (see *Zeus*)

K

Klymene 130
Knossos 60

ACKNOWLEDGMENTS

PICTURE CREDITS
The publisher would like to thank the following
individuals and organizations for their kind
permission to reproduce the images in this
book. Every effort has been made to acknowledge
the pictures. However, we apologize if there
are any omissions.

Ian W. Scott: 20.